DOGS in KNITS

Judith L. Swartz

INTERWEAVE PRESS

Editorial Directors: Betsy Armstrong, Marilyn Murphy
Editor: Elaine Lipson
Technical Editor: Jean Lampe
Proofreader: Nancy Arndt
Illustrations: Gayle Ford, Marjorie C. Leggitt (page 12), Susan Strawn Bailey
Photography: Joe Coca
Cover and interior design: Bren Frisch
Production: Jason Reid, Dean Howes, Marc McCoy Owens
Photo Styling: Linda Ligon, Ann Swanson
Dog quotes: Linda Ligon, Susan Clotfelter

Special thanks to all the humans who so generously shared their beautiful,
well-behaved, supermodel dogs with us: Paula Baum, Sharon Buchele, Laura
Cash, Ann Marie Cole, Jamie Encinia, Reenie and John Hart, Carol Leonard, Day
Ligon, Linda Ligon, Linda and Alan Stark, and Lynn Thor.

Text copyright © 2002 Judith Swartz
Photography copyright © 2002 Joe Coca and Interweave Press, Inc.

Interweave Press, Inc.
201 East Fourth Street
Loveland, Colorado 80537
www.interweave.com

Printed and bound in China through Asia Pacific Offset

Library of Congress Cataloging-in-Publication Data

Swartz, Judith L., 1953–
  Dogs in knits : 17 patterns for our best friends / Judith L. Swartz.
    p. cm.
Includes index.
 ISBN 1-931499-05-5
 1. Knitting—Patterns. 2. Crocheting—Patterns. 3. Dogs—Equipment
and supplies. 4. Sweaters. I. Title.
 TT825 .S885 2002
 746.43'2043--dc21
                              2002000055

First printing: 15M:202:APO

acknowledgements This book is dedicated to my parents, Claire and Alex Swartz, who have always encouraged me to do what I love.

Special thanks go out to many people who helped to make this book possible. A very special thanks goes out to my husband, Joel Marcus, for his love, support, patience, and understanding, and for allowing me the time I needed to complete this book. I look forward to resuming our evening dog walks.

Special thanks to our dog, Tova, my muse and test-marketer.

Many thanks to my good friend Marilyn Murphy, a woman of great vision, who helped make this project possible and who throughout our friendship has always helped me to realize my own visions and stretch beyond my expectations. Thanks to Elaine Lipson for her superb editing abilities and for her hard work, friendship, encouragement, and support throughout this project. Thanks to Linda Ligon for finding just the right dogs to model the sweaters and to Jean Lampe for her meticulous technical editing. Thanks to the staff at Interweave Press for all their behind-the-scenes efforts in making this book possible. Thanks to Don Greenwood for his back cover photography.

My appreciation goes out to all the yarn companies who so generously supplied the wonderful yarns for this book. It's always a pleasure to work with fine materials.

I would like to acknowledge all the "fit models" who so graciously tried on sweaters and let me measure them: Lily, Tova, Nick, Sydney, Madeline, Joe, Emmy, and Pookie. And last but not least, my cat, Charlotte, who stood in when the dogs were busy and, as always, remained a good sport.

TABLE OF CONTENTS

Introduction

When I was eight years old, I adopted my first dog and I learned how to knit. These two highly auspicious but seemingly disparate events have shaped the fabric of my life. Some forty years later, it has been a great labor of love to write a book honoring and combining my two greatest passions.

It's hard to articulate the great love I have for both dogs and knitting, and why they enrich my life so enormously. It sounds simplistic to say that dogs make me happy, but I know that dogs touch something in the very core of me. Knitting not only gives me great pleasure, it keeps me centered and calms me. As a designer, I am always "thinking in sweaters."

It's been a delightful challenge to "think in dog sweaters." I've had to ask myself what dogs would want. It might sound a little pretentious to say that I wanted to create serious garments and accessories for dogs, because—by their very nature—sweaters for dogs can only be so serious. But I did want to create garments that dogs can wear happily, heads and tails high with pride. I wanted to avoid silly costumes and create classic pieces that dogs can wear with dignity.

As I looked to traditional and ethnic knitting and textile patterns and techniques for inspiration, my challenge was to adapt them to a canine format, abstracting for the smaller scale but still maintaining the integrity of the design in a non-exploitive way. As a result, the projects in this book represent a comprehensive sampling of traditional knitting styles. New or less experienced knitters can sample techniques such as Fair Isle, cables, and intarsia without committing to a human-sized project.

I want to thank everyone who has offered wonderful ideas for other "creature comforts" to include. A few of those—a recipe for natural dog treats, a formula for an herbal flea oil—are in these pages. Our dogs give so much to us, and ask for so little in return, that it is a pleasure to create a collection that goes beyond wearables to include other little goodies for our dogs' happiness and well-being.

And because the world as we know it changed as this book came to fruition, we've also included a short tribute to the rescue and therapy dogs who contribute so much to the lives of those in crisis. I am pleased to honor the intelligence and integrity of the rescue dogs who work so tirelessly, as well as the compassion and friendship of all the dogs that readers of this book care for, knit for, and love.

ALL SWEATERS IN THIS BOOK HAVE BEEN WRITTEN FOR FOUR SIZES:

SMALL: Puppies and small dogs under 10 pounds in weight

MEDIUM: Dogs from about 12 to 20 pounds

LARGE: Dogs from about 25 to 40 pounds

EXTRA LARGE: Dogs from about 45 to 75 pounds.

How To Measure Your Dog

Dogs come in so many shapes and sizes that it's impossible to create universally fitting patterns. The patterns in this book are designed to fit average dog body types, but it's best to take key measurements and adjust accordingly to ensure a custom fit for your dog. Since being measured is not an event dogs are accustomed to, keep a few little treats handy and also let your dog inspect the tape measure (especially if it is a spring type) before starting.

There are five key measurements that determine a good fit (see page 9, top, for instructions). Each pattern lists chest circumference and length for the finished garments, and schematic drawings are shown for each garment, so you can

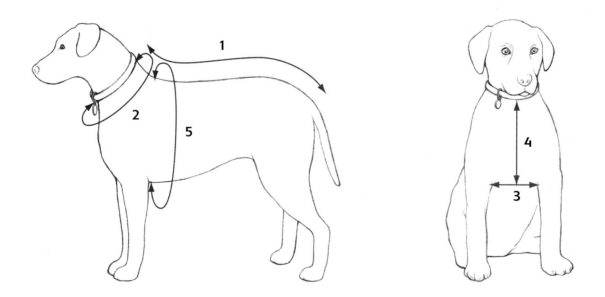

1 ■ LENGTH:

Measure down the center back of your dog from just below the collar to just above the base of the tail. Sweaters can be shorter than this length, depending on style, but never longer.

Georgia 15"
- 12-05

2 ■ NECK CIRCUMFERENCE:

Measure around your dog's neck just below the collar. Add about one inch (2.5 cm) for ease. The next two measurements will help determine correct placement of leg openings.

 10½"

3 ■ WIDTH BETWEEN FRONT LEGS:

Measure between the front legs at the top of the legs (where the front legs meet the body). No additional ease is necessary with this measurement.

3¾

4 ■ LENGTH FROM NECK TO LEG OPENINGS:

Measure at center front, straight down from neck to top of front legs. No additional ease is necessary with this measurement.

 4"

5 ■ CHEST CIRCUMFERENCE:

Measure around the widest part, generally just behind the front legs. Depending on the desired fit of the sweater (close fitting, loose fitting or oversized) add from one to five inches (2.5 to 12.5 cm) of ease.

17"

---

compare your dog's individual measurements.

My intention isn't to discriminate against dogs larger than 75 pounds, but they are less likely to wear sweaters. Using the above measurements, you can adapt many of these patterns for a larger dog. Some additional tips for adjusting patterns as needed:

- It is generally easier to adjust length than width, so if your dog is shorter and wider go to the larger size and make it shorter.

- If your dog's measurements fall between sizes, it is sometimes possible to adjust needle sizes slightly (up or down one size) to gain or lose an inch or two, depending on total number of stitches. If you try this, I recommend making some careful cal-

culations first. A gauge swatch (see Glossary, page 10) is your best tool. Divide the number of stitches in the pattern by the actual number of stitches per inch to determine the width. For example, if the actual gauge of the pattern is 16 stitches = 4" (10 cm) on a size 8 (5 mm) needle (4 stitches to the inch) and the pattern calls for 80 stitches, the garment would then measure 20" (51 cm). By going up a needle size, the gauge might change to 15 stitches = 4", an 80-stitch piece would then measure 21½" (about 54 cm). Conversely, a size 7 (4.5 mm) needle might yield 17 stitches = 4", and then 80 stitches would measure 18¾" (47.5 cm). This might be all the adjustment you need for a better

fit, but it is best to work up swatches and measure carefully.

- In patterns where row gauge is important, you may want to stay with a predetermined pattern.

- Careful measuring of both dog and gauge swatch are the keys to well-fitting, comfortable garments that your dog can enjoy for many years.

Glossary of Abbreviations and Techniques

beg	beginning; begin; begins
bet	between
BO	bind off
CC	contrasting color
CD	central decrease—slip 2 st tog knitwise, k1, pass slipped stitches over the k stitch
ch	chain
cm	centimeter(s)
cn	cable needle
CO	cast on
cont	continue
dc	double crochet
dec(s)	decrease(s); decreasing
dpn	double-pointed needle(s)
foll	following
fwd	forward
g	gram(s)
hdc	half double crochet
inc	increase(s); increasing
k	knit
k1f&b	knit into front and back of same st
k tbl	knit through back loop
k2tog	knit two stitches together
kwise	knitwise
m	In pattern instructions, refers to marker(s); in yarn yardage specifications, refers to meter(s).
M1	make one stitch by lifting the horizontal running thread between two stitches and knitting into the back of it
M1-left slant	Make one, left slant. With left needle tip, pick up running strand between 2 sts from front to back, knit strand through the back loop to twist.
M1-right slant	Make one, right slant. With left needle tip, pick up running strand between 2 sts from back to front, knit strand through the front loop to twist.
MC	main color
mm	millimeter(s)
p	purl
p1f&b	purl into front and back of same stitch
p tbl	purl through back loop
patt(s)	pattern(s)
pm	place marker
psso	pass slipped stitch over
p2tog	purl two stitches together
pwise	purlwise
rem	remaining
rep	repeat
rev St st	reverse stockinette stitch
rib	ribbing
rnd(s)	round(s)
RS	right side
rsc	reverse single crochet
sc	single crochet
sk	skip
sl	slip
sl st	slip stitch (purlwise unless otherwise indicated)
ssk	slip 1 knitwise, slip 1 knitwise, k2 sl sts tog tbl
ssp	slip 1 kwise, slip 1 kwise, p2 sl sts tog tbl
st(s)	stitch(es)
St st	stockinette stitch
tbl	through the back loop
tog	together
WS	wrong side
wyb	with yarn in back
wyf	with yarn in front
yd	yard(s)
yo	yarn over

*	repeat starting point (i.e. repeat from *)
* *	repeat all instructions between asterisks
( )	alternate measurements and/or instructions
[ ]	instructions that are to be worked as a group a specified number of times

Knitting Gauge

To check gauge, cast on 30 to 40 stitches using recommended needle size. Work in pattern stitch until piece measures at least 4″ (10 cm) from cast-on edge. Remove swatch from needles or bind off loosely, and lay swatch on flat surface. Place a ruler over swatch and count number of stitches across and number of rows down (including fractions of stitches and rows) in 4″ (10 cm). Repeat two or three times on different areas of swatch to confirm measurements. If you have more stitches and rows than called for in instructions, use larger needles; if you have fewer, use smaller needles. Repeat until gauge is correct.

Reading Charts

Unless otherwise indicated, read charts from the bottom up. On right-side rows, read charts from right to left. On wrong-side rows, read charts from left to right. When knitting in the round, read charts from right to left for all rows.

Make 1 (M1) Increase

With left needle tip, lift the strand between last knitted stitch and first stitch on left needle, from front to back (Figure 1). Knit the lifted loop through back (Figure 2).

Figure 1

Figure 2

Ssk Decrease

Slip two stitches knitwise one at a time (Figure 1). Insert point of left needle into front of two slipped stitches and knit them together through back loops with right needle (Figure 2).

Figure 1

Figure 2

Continental (Long-Tail) Cast-On

Make a slipknot and place on right-hand needle, leaving a long tail. Place thumb and index finger of left hand between the two threads. Secure long ends with your other three fingers. Hold your hand palm up and spread thumb and index finger apart to make a V of yarn around them. There are four strands of yarn, 1, 2, 3, and 4 (Figure 1). Place needle under strand 1, from front to back. Place needle over top of strand 3 (Figure 2) and bring needle down through loop around thumb (Figure 3). Drop loop off thumb and, placing thumb back in the V configuration, tighten up resulting stitch on needle.

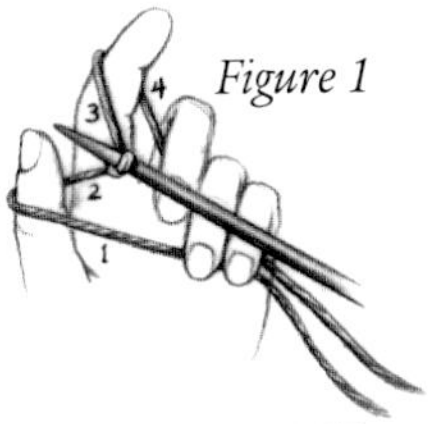

Figure 1

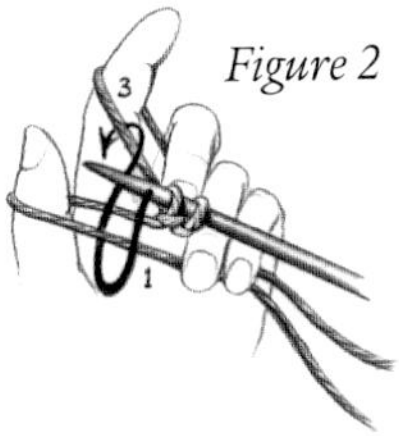

Figure 2

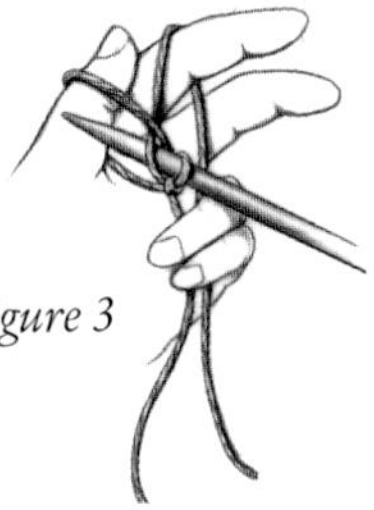

Figure 3

Stranding Methods for 2-Color Knitting

Knit rows

Use your left hand to keep the pattern color below the tip of the left needle while your right forefinger brings the background color around the tip of the right needle to knit the stitch. Repeat this until the colors change.

Use your left forefinger to bring the pattern yarn around the needle and use the tip of the needle to draw the new stitch through while your right hand keeps the background color away from the needle tip and above the other stitches.

Right hand knits with background color, left hand carries pattern color.

Right finger keeps background color above pattern color.

Left hand holds pattern color under stitch being purled.

Right hand holds background color away from needle tips.

Purl rows

The purl row, although a little more difficult to learn, is worked the same way. Use your left hand to keep the pattern yarn below the purled stitches when it is not being worked.

Use your right hand to hold the background yarn up and away from the needle tips while your left forefinger passes the pattern yarn around the needle tip.

Intarsia

Use this method to work small areas of different colors without forming holes. These areas can be worked with small balls of the color wound onto bobbins and twisted over the adjacent color at every color join. Small areas can be worked with a loose length of yarn.

Work to the color change, then bring the color that has been used over the new color, and bring the new color up so that the yarns link or are twisted at the joining point.

Where irregular shapes are worked in the same design, you may need to carry some colors without working them for a number of stitches by weaving them in along the back. Look ahead one or two rows of the intarsia chart to decide where to position the yarn in preparation for the next row.

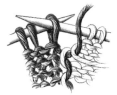

Twist one yarn over the other on the wrong side.

Back Stitch

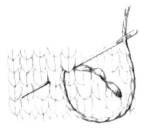

Bring threaded needle out from back to front between the first two knitted stitches you want to cover. *Insert needle at the right edge of the right stitch and bring it back out at the left edge of the remaining stitch. Insert needle again between the first two stitches and bring it out between the next two to be covered. Repeat from *. The stitches can be worked in any direction.

Blanket Stitch

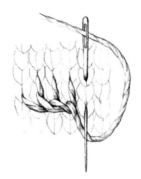

Bring threaded needle out from back to front at the center of a knitted stitch. *Insert needle at center of next stitch to the right and two rows up, and out at the center of the stitch two rows below. Repeat from *.

French Knot

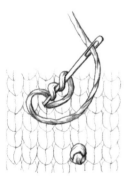

Bring needle out of knitted background from back to front, wrap yarn around needle one to three times, and use thumb to hold in place while pulling needle through wraps into background a short distance from where it came out.

Chain Stitch

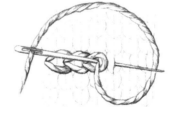

Bring threaded needle out from back to front at center of a knitted stitch. Form a short loop and insert needle back where it came out. Keeping the loop under the needle, bring needle back out in center of next stitch to the right.

Feather Stitch

Bring threaded needle from back to front and make a loose stitch to the left, forming an open loop. Bring needle up at middle of first stitch at loop's lowest point, then take next stitch forming a loop to the right. Continue alternating loops to the right and left to form feather-like stitch.

Single Crochet (sc)

Figure 1   *Figure 2*

Insert the hook into a stitch, yarn over hook and draw a loop through stitch, yarn over hook (Figure 1) and draw it through both loops on hook (Figure 2).

Half-double Crochet (hdc)

Figure 1   *Figure 2*

Take yarn over the hook, insert the hook into a stitch, yarn over the hook and draw a loop through the stitch (3 loops on hook), yarn over the hook and draw it through all the loops on the hook.

Standard Bind-Off

This is the most common, and for many knitters, the only method for binding off. Use this method for edges that will be sewn into seams or finished in some way (such as stitches being picked up and knitted).

Slip 1 stitch, *knit 1 stitch, insert left needle tip into first stitch on right needle (Figure 1), pass this stitch over the second stitch (Figure 2), and off the needle—1 stitch remains on right needle and 1 stitch has been bound off (Figure 3). Repeat from *.

Figure 1   *Figure 2*   *Figure 3*

Double Crochet (dc)

Figure 1   *Figure 2*

Yarn over hook, insert hook into a stitch, yarn over hook and draw a loop through (three loops on hook), yarn over hook (Figure 1) and draw it through two loops, yarn over hook and draw it through the remaining two loops (Figure 2).

Reverse Single Crochet (rev sc)

Working from left to right, insert crochet hook into a knit edge stitch, draw up a loop, bring yarn over hook, and draw this loop through the first one. *Insert hook into next stitch to right (Figure 1), draw up a loop, bring yarn over hook again (Figure 2), and draw this loop through both loops on hook (Figure 3); repeat from *.

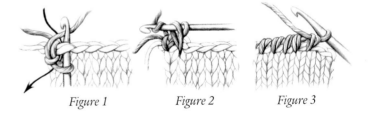

Figure 1   *Figure 2*   *Figure 3*

Crochet Chain (ch)

Make a slipknot on hook. Yarn over hook and draw it through loop of the slipknot. Repeat, drawing yarn through the last loop formed.

Perfect Pom-Pon

1. Cut two cardboard circles ½″ (1.3 cm) larger in diameter than the desired finished size. Cut a ¾″ (2-cm) hole in the center of each circle. Cut away a small wedge of each circle to make it easier to wrap the yarn. Place a tie strand of yarn between the circles and hold them together, with both openings together. Wrap yarn around the circles the desired number of times (the more wraps, the thicker the pom-pon).

Figure 1

2. Insert scissors between circles and carefully cut around the outer edge to release the yarn. Knot the tie strand tightly around the group of yarn. Gently ease the cardboard from the pom-pon.

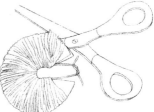

Figure 2

3. Cut two cardboard circles ½″ (1.3 cm) smaller than the first two (the diameter of the desired finished size). Poke a pinpoint hole in the center of each circle. Sandwich the pom-pon between these two circles and insert a long tapestry needle through the hole in one circle, though the center of the pom-pon and out through the hole in the other circle. This will hold the pom-pon in place as you trim around the edges of the circles to even out the pom-pon.

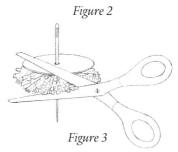

Figure 3

Kitchener Stitch

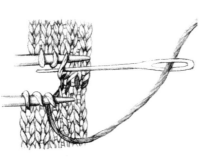

Step 1: Bring threaded needle through front stitch as if to purl and leave stitch on needle.

Step 2: Bring threaded needle through back stitch as if to knit and leave stitch on needle.

Step 3: Bring threaded needle through the same front stitch as if to knit and slip this stitch off needle. Bring threaded needle through next front stitch as if to purl and leave stitch on needle.

Step 4: Bring threaded needle through first back stitch as if to purl (as illustrated), slip that stitch off, bring needle through next back stitch as if to knit, leave this stitch on needle.

Repeat Steps 3 and 4 until no stitches remain on needles.

Duplicate Stitch

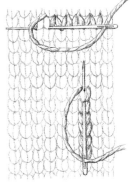

Horizontal: Bring threaded needle out from back to front at the base of the V of the knitted stitch you want to cover. *Working right to left, pass needle in and out under the stitch in the row above it and back into the base of the same stitch. Bring needle back out at the base of the V of the next stitch to the left. Repeat from *.

Vertical: Beginning at lowest point, work as for horizontal duplicate stitch, ending by bringing the needle back out at the base of the stitch directly above the stitch just worked.

I-Cord

With double-pointed needle, cast on desired number of stitches. *Without turning the needle, slide the stitches to other end of the needle, pull the yarn around the back, and knit the stitches as usual; repeat from * for desired length.

Attached I-Cord

As I-cord is knitted, attach it to the garment as follows: With garment RS facing and using a separate ball of yarn and circular needle, pick up the desired number of stitches along the garment edge. Slide these stitches down the needle so that the first picked-up stitch is near the opposite needle point. With double-pointed needle, cast on desired number of I-cord stitches. Knit across the I-cord to the last stitch, then knit the last stitch together with the first picked-up stitch on the garment, and pull the yarn behind the cord. Knit to the last I-cord stitch, then knit the last I-cord stitch together with the next picked-up stitch. Continue in this manner until all picked-up stitches have been used.

Inserting a Zipper

Preshrink the zipper and finish the edge of the knitted fabric by folding the edge stitch to the wrong side. Working from the right side and beginning at the base, pin each side of closed zipper to wrong side of knitted fabric so folded edges come together and hide teeth. Keep zipper flat and at the same position on both sides.

With contrasting thread, baste zipper in place close to teeth (Figure 1). Remove pins. Turn work over and use coordinating thread to whipstitch edges of zipper to wrong side of knitted fabric (Figure 2). Turn work back to right side. With coordinating thread and using a backstitch, sew zipper to knitted fabric close to teeth (Figure 3).

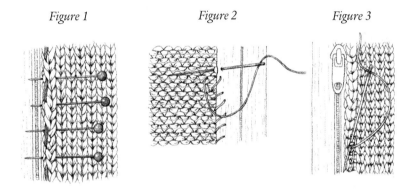

Figure 1   *Figure 2*   *Figure 3*

3 (4, 5) Stitch One-Row Buttonhole

Work to where you want the buttonhole to begin, bring yarn to front, slip 1 purlwise, bring yarn to back (Figure 1). *Slip 1 purlwise, pass first slipped stitch over second; rep from * 2 (3, 4) more times. Place last stitch back on left needle (Figure 2), turn. Cast on 4 (5, 6) stitches as follows: *Insert right needle between the first and second stitches on left needle, draw up a loop, and place it on the left needle (Figure 3); rep from * 3 (4, 5) more times, turn. Bring yarn to back, slip first stitch of left needle onto right needle and pass last cast-on stitch over it (Figure 4), work to end of row.

Figure 1

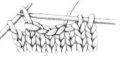

Figure 2

Figure 3

Figure 4

BAXTER

Big dogs, little dogs,
black dogs, white dogs,
we all need sweaters
for a dog party.
To the tree!
To the tree!
—*with apologies to*
P. D. Eastman

Basic Knitted
Dog Sweater

This is a basic stockinette stitch sweater with rib trim. It is intended to be close-fitting, with only a small amount of ease.

SIZE

FINISHED SIZE

YARN

NOTIONS

NEEDLES

GAUGE

SIZE
S (M, L, XL) to fit chest 14 (18, 22, 26)" (35.5 [46, 56, 66] cm).

FINISHED SIZE
14½ (19, 24½, 28)" (37 [48.5, 62, 71] cm) chest circumference; 12 (16, 21, 23)" (30.5 [40.5, 53.5, 58.5] cm) length. Sweater shown in all sizes.

YARN
Worsted weight yarn, approximately 220 (440, 440, 660) yd (201 [402, 402, 604] m).

NEEDLES
Size 7 (4.5 mm): set of 5 double-pointed needles (dpn) and 24" (61 cm) circular needle; size 5 (3.75 mm): set of 5 double pointed needles and 24" (61 cm) circular needle. **Optional:** Size 5 (3.75mm) 16" (40.5cm) circular needle. Adjust needle sizes if necessary to obtain the correct gauge.

NOTIONS
Stitch holder; tapestry needle.

GAUGE
18 sts and 25 rows = 4" (10 cm) in St st; 26 sts and 26 rows = 4" (10 cm) in k1, p1 rib (un-stretched).

Basic Knitted Dog Sweater

NOTE
We used Cascade Yarns Cascade 220 worsted weight yarn (see Yarns, page 94).

BACK
Starting at neck edge with larger needles, CO 48 (66, 88, 98) sts. Work back and forth in St st for 8 (12, 16, 18)" (20.5 [30.5, 40.5, 46] cm), ending with WS row. *Note:* Work following decs one stitch in from each edge. Dec 1 st each edge every other row 9 (11, 9, 14) times, then every third row 0 (0, 3, 0) times—30 (44, 64, 70) sts rem. When work measures 12 (16, 21, 23)" (30.5 [40.5, 53.5, 58.5] cm) from beg, BO all sts.

UNDERPANEL
With larger needles, CO 7 sts. Working in k1, p1 rib, inc 1 st each edge every other row 0 (0, 0, 3) times, then every third row 7 (9, 13, 14) times—21 (25, 33, 41) sts on needle. Work even until panel measures 8 (12, 16, 18)" (20.5 [30.5, 40.5, 46] cm) from CO edge. Place sts on holder.

FINISHING
Sew underpanel to sides of back, matching length of under panel to straight edge of back, leaving a 2 (2½, 3, 3½)" (5 [6.5, 7.5, 9] cm) opening in seam starting 3½ (5, 7, 8)" (9 [12.5, 15, 20.5] cm) from neck edge. (This should be just where the underpanel reaches its widest point.) *Neck:* With dpn and RS facing pick up 52 (64, 72, 82) sts evenly around neck edge. Work ¾"(2 cm) in k1, p1 rib for crew-neck style, or 1½" (3.8 cm) for mock turtleneck, or 3" (7.5 cm) for turtleneck. Bind off all sts loosely. *Leg openings:* With dpn pick up 24 (28, 30, 36) sts evenly around leg opening. Work 5 rnds in k1, p1 rib. Bind off all sts. *Bottom edge:* With smaller size 24" circ needle (or dpn for smallest size sweater) pick up 82 (110, 136, 166) sts around lower edge, including held sts of underpanel. Maintaining est rib patt of underpanel, work 5 rnds in k1, p1 rib. Bind off loosely.

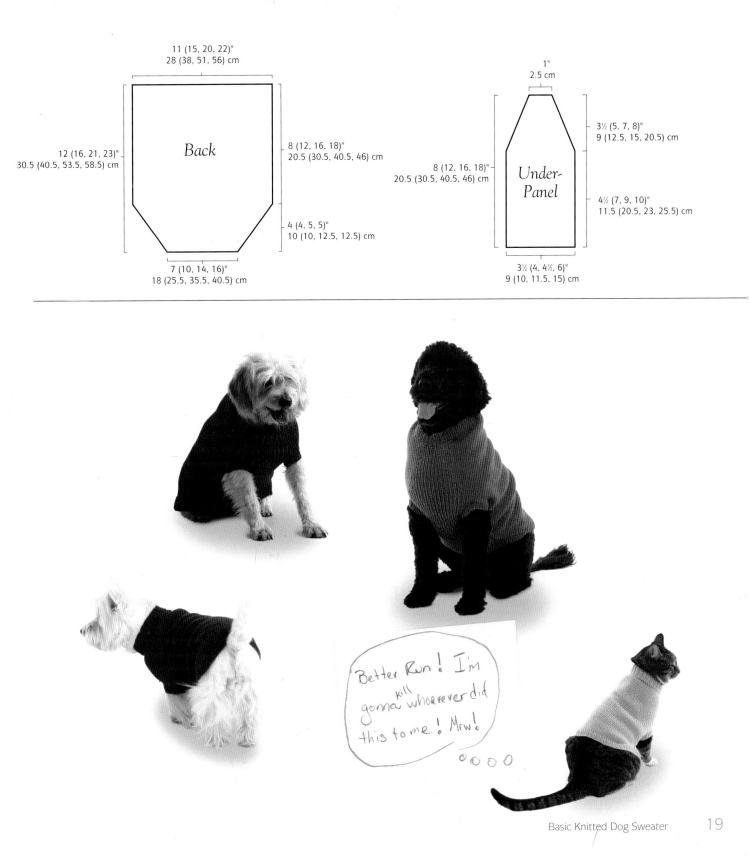

11 (15, 20, 22)"
28 (38, 51, 56) cm

Back

12 (16, 21, 23)"
30.5 (40.5, 53.5, 58.5) cm

8 (12, 16, 18)"
20.5 (30.5, 40.5, 46) cm

4 (4, 5, 5)"
10 (10, 12.5, 12.5) cm

7 (10, 14, 16)"
18 (25.5, 35.5, 40.5) cm

1"
2.5 cm

3½ (5, 7, 8)"
9 (12.5, 15, 20.5) cm

Under-Panel

8 (12, 16, 18)"
20.5 (30.5, 40.5, 46) cm

4½ (7, 9, 10)"
11.5 (20.5, 23, 25.5) cm

3½ (4, 4½, 6)"
9 (10, 11.5, 15) cm

LILY

Being all hooks at fiber arts is no excuse to let your dog go sweaterless. I like this crocheted sweater as much as I like curling up on my warm afghan (and I hope that this little corner I chewed doesn't show).

Basic Crocheted Dog Sweater

Beginners will enjoy this very basic pattern, while more experienced crocheters can use it as a framework to expand upon or embellish. It is a close-fitting sweater.

SIZE	FINISHED SIZE	YARN	NEEDLES	GAUGE
S (M, L, XL) to fit chest 14 (18, 22, 26)" (35.5 [46, 56, 66] cm).	15 (19, 25, 29)" (38 [48.5, 63.5, 73.5] cm) chest circumference; 12 (16, 21, 23)" (30.5 [40.5, 53.5, 58.5] cm) length. Sweater shown is Medium, 16" chest.	Worsted weight yarn, approximately 300 (350, 450, 550) yd (275 [320, 412, 503] m).	Size H/8 (5.0 mm) crochet hook. Adjust hook size if necessary to obtain the correct gauge.	16 sts and 16 rows = 4" (10 cm) in single crochet (sc); 20 sts and 10 rows = 5" (12.75 cm) in half double crochet (hdc).

Basic Crocheted Dog Sweater

NOTES
We used Cascade Yarns Cascade 220 worsted weight yarn (see Yarns, page 94).
For crochet stitch abbreviations, see page 13.

BACK
Beg at lower edge, with size H/8 (5.0 mm) crochet hook, ch 32 (40, 56, 64) plus 2 ch for turning sts. Working in hdc, work 2 rows even beg in third chain from hook. Cont in hdc, inc 1 st each edge every row 4 (8, 9, 9) times, then every other row 2 (0, 1, 1) times—44 (56, 76, 84) sts, to measure 11 (14, 19, 21)" (28 [35.5, 48.5, 53.5] cm) wide. Work even until back measures a total length of 12 (16, 21, 23)" (30.5 [40.5, 53.5, 58.5] cm). Fasten off.

UNDERPANEL
With size H/8 (5.00 mm) crochet hook, ch 5. Work 1 row sc (4 sts). Cont in sc, inc 1 st each edge every other row 5 (7, 6, 10) times, then every third row 1 (1, 4, 4) times—16 (20, 24, 32) sts, to measure 4 (5, 6, 8)" (10 [12.5, 15, 20.5] cm) wide. Work even until underpanel measures 8 (12, 16, 18)" (20.5 [30.5, 40.5, 46] cm) in length from beg. Fasten off.

FINISHING
Sew back to underpanel along side edges, leaving a 2½ (3, 3, 3½)" (6.5 [7.5, 7.5, 9] cm) leg opening, beg where underpanel reaches its widest point and matching side edges with those of back to the point where it begins to narrow. *Lower edge:* Work 1 row sc, evenly spacing approximately 78 (92, 120, 136) sts around lower edge. Work 1 row reverse single crochet (see Glossary, page 13). *Neck edge:* Work 5 rows sc, evenly spacing approximately 44 (56, 76, 84) sts evenly around neck edge. Work 1 row reverse single crochet. *Leg openings:* Work 2 rows sc around leg openings, evenly spacing 20 (24, 24, 28) sts around opening. Work 1 row reverse single crochet. Block or steam sweater to size.

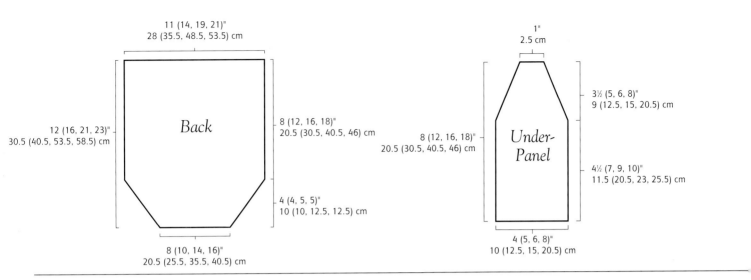

11 (14, 19, 21)"
28 (35.5, 48.5, 53.5) cm

Back

12 (16, 21, 23)"
30.5 (40.5, 53.5, 58.5) cm

8 (12, 16, 18)"
20.5 (30.5, 40.5, 46) cm

4 (4, 5, 5)"
10 (10, 12.5, 12.5) cm

8 (10, 14, 16)"
20.5 (25.5, 35.5, 40.5) cm

1"
2.5 cm

Under-Panel

3½ (5, 6, 8)"
9 (12.5, 15, 20.5) cm

8 (12, 16, 18)"
20.5 (30.5, 40.5, 46) cm

4½ (7, 9, 10)"
11.5 (20.5, 23, 25.5) cm

4 (5, 6, 8)"
10 (12.5, 15, 20.5) cm

Most Popular Dog Names

In North America, the most popular dog names are:

1. Sam, Sammie, or Samantha
2. Max, Maxie, Maxwell or Maxine
3. Lady
4. Bear
5. Maggie
6. Buddy
7. Tasha
8. Chelsea
9. Holly
10. Shasta

Source: www.petrix.com

CHARLEY

For a long, low dog like me, struggling into a conventional sweater isn't always a top-notch time. This get-up suits my dignity—I was, after all, for one brief shining moment, a sire to show dogs. This sweater thing is just sporty enough to remind my human that I'm craving a high-speed scamper in the autumn leaves.

Garter Stitch Topper with Easy Embroidery

This simple sweater pays homage to my first real knitting project—a sweater for Duchess, my first dog. In easy garter stitch with simple backstitch embroidery, this topper offers an alternative to sweaters that must be pulled over the dog's head.

SIZE
S (M, L, XL) to fit chest 14 (16, 22, 26)" (35.5 [40.5, 56, 66] cm).

FINISHED SIZE
12 (14, 20, 22)" (30.5 [35.5, 51, 56] cm) across back; 12 (16, 22, 24)" (30.5 [40.5, 56, 61] cm) length. Size shown is Medium, 14" (35.5 cm) across back.

YARN
Worsted weight yarn, approximately 350 (400, 450, 500) yd (320 [366, 412, 458] m) blue-gray; 10 yd (9.2 m) of contrasting yarn in similar weight for embroidery.

NEEDLES
Size 6 (4 mm) and size 7 (4.5 mm). Adjust needle sizes if necessary to obtain the correct gauge.

NOTIONS
Tapestry needle for embroidery; two 1" (2.5 cm) buttons; one ¾" (2 cm) button.

GAUGE
20 sts and 40 rows = 4" (10 cm) on size 7 (4.5 mm) needles in garter stitch (knit every row).

Garter Stitch Topper with Easy Embroidery

NOTES
We used Lane Borgosesia Maratona merino wool yarn (see Yarns, page 94).

To determine length of neck and chest bands for individual dogs, it is best to measure around neck and add 1" (2.5 cm) to actual measurement; also measure around widest part of chest and add 1" (2.5 cm) to actual measurement. There is quite a bit of stretch to the garter stitch bands, so err a little on the short side rather than having bands that are too long.

BACK
Beg at neck edge with size 7 (4.5 mm) needles, CO 50 (60, 80, 90) sts. Knit 1 row. Next row (inc row): K4, M1, k to last 4 sts, M1, k to end. Working in garter st (knit every row), rep inc row every fourth row, 5 times total for both Small and Medium sizes, or every third row 10 times total for Large and X-Large sizes—60 (70, 100, 110) sts. Work even until piece measures 10 (14, 19, 21)" (25.5 [35.5, 48.5, 53.5] cm) from CO edge, ending with a WS row. Next row (dec row): K3, k2tog, k to last 5 sts, k2tog, k3. Cont in garter st, rep dec row every fourth row for 10 (10, 15, 15) times total. Work 4 rows even. Bind off remaining 40 (50, 70, 80) sts loosely.

NECK BAND
With size 6 (4 mm) needles, CO 3 sts. Work in garter st, inc 1 st each edge every other row 2 times—7 sts. Cont in garter st, sl first st of each row with yarn in back (wyb). Work even until band is 11 (13, 20, 22)" (28 [33, 51, 56] cm) long.

Work 3-st buttonhole on next row (see Glossary, page 15). Cont in garter st, dec 1 st each edge every other row 2 times. Bind off rem 3 sts.

CHEST BAND
(Make 2) With size 6 (4 mm) needles, CO 5 sts. Work in garter st, inc 1 st each edge every other row 2 times—9 sts. Work even in garter st to a total length of 16 (20, 26, 28)" (40.5 [51, 66, 71] cm), sl the first st of each row wyb. Work a 3-st buttonhole on next row. Cont in garter st, dec 1 st each edge every other row 2 times. Bind off rem 5 sts.

FINISHING
Embroidery: With contrast yarn work backstitch (see Glossary, page 12) along outer edges of back approximately ¾" (2 cm) from edge, using

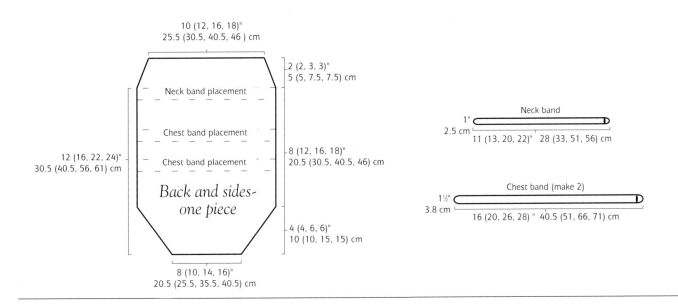

10 (12, 16, 18)"
25.5 (30.5, 40.5, 46) cm

2 (2, 3, 3)"
5 (5, 7.5, 7.5) cm

Neck band placement

Chest band placement

12 (16, 22, 24)"
30.5 (40.5, 56, 61) cm

Chest band placement

8 (12, 16, 18)"
20.5 (30.5, 40.5, 46) cm

*Back and sides-
one piece*

4 (4, 6, 6)"
10 (10, 15, 15) cm

8 (10, 14, 16)"
20.5 (25.5, 35.5, 40.5) cm

Neck band

1"
2.5 cm

11 (13, 20, 22)" 28 (33, 51, 56) cm

Chest band (make 2)

1½"
3.8 cm

16 (20, 26, 28) " 40.5 (51, 66, 71) cm

garter ridges and inc/dec lines as guides and reversing RS/WS of work at collar. Embroider along edges of neck and chest bands. ***Neck and chest bands:*** Thread tapestry needle with matching yarn. Center neck band under collar and tack in place at center. Fold collar over band and tack with 1 stitch through all layers. Place one chest band 4 (5, 7, 8)″ (10 [12.5, 18, 20.5] cm) down from neck band with buttonhole aligned with right edge of topper back. Tack in place at center back, left edge and above buttonhole at right edge. Place second chest band 1″ (2.5 cm) down from first and tack in place the same way. Sew smaller button to neckband at opposite end of buttonhole and larger buttons to chest bands at ends opposite buttonholes.

"I think we are drawn to dogs because they are the uninhibited creatures we might be if we weren't certain we knew better."

—George Bird Evans

MAGGIE

A busy West Highland white terrier like me needs room to cavort, and a bright color to set off my lovely white coat. This everyday sweater is perfect sportswear for a gal with impeccable fashion sense and an active lifestyle.

Soft Basketweave Cardigan

This sweater is meant to fit a bit loosely, like a comfy and comforting sweater. The basketweave stitch is easy to learn, making this design perfect for a beginning knitter. One-piece construction keeps finishing to a minimum, and the soft alpaca yarn adds significantly to the coziness.

SIZE
S (M, L, XL) to fit chest 14 (16, 22, 26)" (35.5 [40.5, 56, 66] cm).

FINISHED SIZE
16 (21, 27, 31)" (40.5 [53.5, 68.5, 79] cm) chest circumference. 12 (16, 21, 23)" (30.5 [40.5, 53.5, 58.5] cm) finished length. Sweater shown is Medium, 21" chest.

YARN
Sport weight yarn, approximately 480 (600, 720, 840) yd (439 [549, 659, 768] m).

NEEDLES
Size 6 (4 mm): straight and double-pointed (dpn); size 8 (5 mm). Adjust needle sizes if necessary to obtain the correct gauge.

NOTIONS
Stitch markers (m); 4 (6, 8, 10) ½" (1.3 cm) buttons.

GAUGE
17 sts and 28 rows = 4" (10 cm) in St st with larger needles and two strands of yarn held together; 18 sts and 28 rows = 4" (10 cm) in basketweave stitch with larger needles and two strands of yarn held together.

Soft Basketweave Cardigan

NOTE
We used two strands of Blue Sky Alpaca 100 percent alpaca sport weight yarn held together (see Yarns, page 94).

STITCHES
Garter Stitch, Row Version
Knit every row.

Garter Stitch, Circular Version
Knit 1 rnd, purl 1 rnd.

Stockinette Stitch (St st)
Row 1: (RS) Knit.
Row 2: (WS) Purl.
Rep these 2 rows for patt.

Basketweave
(multiple of 8 sts + 5, and 8 rows)
Row 1: (RS) Knit.
Row 2: K5, *p3, k5; rep from *.
Row 3: P5, *k3, p5; rep from *.
Row 4: Rep Row 2.
Row 5: Knit.
Row 6: K1, *p3, k5; rep from *, end last rep k1 instead of k5.
Row 7: P1, *k3, p5; rep from *, end last rep p1 instead of p5.
Row 8: Rep Row 6.

BODY
Beg at collar edge with smaller needles and 2 strands of yarn held together, CO 45 (61, 77, 85) sts. Work 2 (2, 2½, 2½)" (5 [5, 6.5, 6.5] cm) in garter st, CO 3 sts at beg and end of last row and inc 8 sts evenly across row—59 (75, 91, 99) sts. Change to larger needles and set up body patt as follows:
Row 1: (RS) K3, place marker (pm), work next 53 (69, 85, 93) sts in Row 1 of basketweave patt, pm, k3.
Row 2: (WS) K3, sl m, work sts between m in Row 2 of basketweave patt, sl m, k3.
Row 3: **Buttonhole row:** K1, yo, k2tog, M1, sl m, work Row 3 of basketweave patt on sts between m, sl m, M1, k3—first buttonhole made and 2 sts inc.

Maintaining first 3 sts and last 3 sts in garter st and sts between markers in basketweave patt, work a M1 increase each side, just before or just after basketweave section every other row 3 (5, 4, 6) more times, then every fourth row 5 (5, 8, 10) times, working inc sts in St st—77 (97, 117, 133) sts. *At the same time,* work a yo buttonhole same as Row 3 every 2" (5 cm) or every 14 rows for a total of 4 (6, 8, 10) buttonholes. *Leg openings:* Maintaining patt as est, work leg openings as follows: When work measures 4 (5, 6, 8)" (10 [12.5, 15, 20.5] cm) from beg of basketweave patt, beg with a RS row, work across 3 garter sts and 9 (11, 13, 17) St sts, attach a second ball of yarn and work across 53 (69, 85, 93) basketweave sts, attach a third ball of yarn and work across rem 9 (11, 13, 17) St sts and 3 garter sts. Cont in this manner for 2½ (3, 3½, 3½)" (6.5 [7.5,

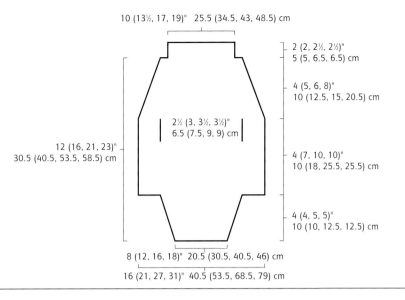

10 (13½, 17, 19)" 25.5 (34.5, 43, 48.5) cm

2 (2, 2½, 2½)"
5 (5, 6.5, 6.5) cm

4 (5, 6, 8)"
10 (12.5, 15, 20.5) cm

2½ (3, 3½, 3½)"
6.5 (7.5, 9, 9) cm

12 (16, 21, 23)"
30.5 (40.5, 53.5, 58.5) cm

4 (7, 10, 10)"
10 (18, 25.5, 25.5) cm

4 (4, 5, 5)"
10 (10, 12.5, 12.5) cm

8 (12, 16, 18)" 20.5 (30.5, 40.5, 46) cm
16 (21, 27, 31)" 40.5 (53.5, 68.5, 79) cm

Dog Facts

There are approximately 68,000,000 owned dogs in the United States.

There are an equal number of male and female dogs owned in the United States.

On average, dog owners have 1.7 dogs.

Source: American Pet Products Manufacturers Association

9, 9] cm), ending with a WS row. Rejoin sections and using one ball of yarn, work even to a total length of 7½ (11½, 15½, 17½)" (19 [29, 39.5, 44.5] cm) from beg of basketweave patt. *Next row:* Work 12 (14, 16, 20) sts in garter st, work center 53 (69, 85, 93) sts in basketweave patt, work last 12 (14, 16, 20) sts in garter st ending with a WS row. When work measures 8 (12, 16, 18)" (20.5 [30.5, 40.5, 46] cm) from beg of bas-

ketweave patt, BO 12 (14, 16, 20) sts at beg of next 2 rows. Cont in basketweave patt, working first 3 sts and last 3 sts in garter st, dec 1 st each edge every fourth row 7 (7, 5, 4) times, then every other row 0 (0, 2, 2) times—39 (55, 71, 81) sts. Work dec as follows: On RS row k3, ssk, work patt sts as est to last 5 sts, k2tog, k3. When work measures 11½ (15½, 20½, 22½)" (29 [39.5, 52, 57] cm) from beg of basket-

weave patt, work all sts in garter st for ½" (1.3 cm). Bind off rem 39 (55, 71, 85) sts loosely.

FINISHING

Leg openings: With smaller dpn pick up 22 (26, 30, 30) sts evenly around leg openings. Work 1" (2.5 cm) in circ garter st. Bind off. ***Buttons:*** Sew buttons on right front button band opposite buttonholes.

Could there be a more
all-American dog than
the beagle? I'm sure
that's why I was chosen
to model this jean
jacket. I feel like such a
dude in this soft cotton
sweater with all its clever
seams and darts. I can
sit up, stand up, roll
over, all those tricks that
make my owner hand
out the treats. Mine is
not to wonder why.

The Jean Jacket
Based on everybody's favorite classic and knitted in an indigo-dyed cotton yarn guaranteed to fade and soften just like real denim fabric, this jacket features details adapted from its human counterpart. This pattern is suitable for intermediate to experienced knitters.

SIZE
S (M, L, XL) to fit chest 14 (16, 22, 26)" (35.5 [40.5, 56, 66] cm).

FINISHED SIZE
16 (21, 27, 30)" (40.5 [53.5, 68.5, 76] cm) chest circumference; 12 (16, 21, 23)" (30.5 [40.5, 53.5, 58.5] cm) length.

Size shown is Medium, 21" (40.5 cm) chest.

YARN
Double knitting weight denim-type yarn, approximately 300 (400, 500, 600) yd (275 [366, 458, 549] m) denim blue.

NEEDLES
Size 4 (3.5 mm): straight and double-pointed needles (dpn); size 6 (4 mm): straight needles. Adjust needle sizes if necessary to obtain the correct gauge.

NOTIONS
2 stitch holders; stitch markers (m); 6 (8, 10, 12) ¾" (2 cm) buttons (we used Dritz No Sew Dungaree buttons).

GAUGE
19 sts and 25 rows = 4" (10 cm) in St st on size 6 (4 mm) needles *before washing*; 19 stitches and 28 rows = 4 inches after *washing*.

The Jean Jacket

NOTES

We used Rowan Denim yarn (see Yarn, page 94), which shrinks in length after washing just like denim fabric. Be sure to knit a sample swatch and wash it (the swatch made for our sample garment was machine-washed and dried) and determine gauge from washed sample. If using a different yarn, make sure gauge swatch corresponds to "after washing" specifications. Note also that length determinations in pattern are written in terms of rows and not inches, making accurate swatch measurement all the more important.

It is the nature of indigo dye to rub off on one's hands while knitting, but any residue washes off easily with soap and water. Wash garment separately or with like colors.

STITCHES

Reverse Stockinette Stitch
P on RS, K on WS.

Garter Stitch, Row Version
Knit all rows.

Garter Stitch, Circular Version
Knit 1 rnd, purl 1 rnd.

BODY

Beg at collar edge with smaller needles, CO 48 (66, 88, 98) sts. Work 14 (16, 20, 24) rows in garter st, inc 8 (10, 10, 10) sts evenly across last row—56 (76, 98, 108) sts. Change to larger needles and work 6 more rows in garter st, casting on 3 sts at beg of first 2 rows—62 (82, 104, 114) sts. On third row (RS), work buttonhole as follows: at beg of row, k2, yo, k2 tog. Rep buttonhole every 16 (14, 14, 12) rows for a total count of 4 (6, 8, 10) buttonholes. On seventh row (RS), beg inc to create underpanel, and *at the same time,* set up patt as follows: K3, M1, pm, work next 56 (76, 98, 108) sts in Reverse St st, pm, M1, k3. Work new sts in St st. Cont M1 inc before or after m every 4 (3, 3, 3) rows 6 (9, 13, 15) times—74 (94, 130, 144) sts. *At the same time,* after 22 (28, 36, 48) rows from 3 st CO have been worked, establish pocket openings across back: on a RS row, work across garter and St sts of underpanel as est, then purl across 10 (19, 24, 26) Reverse St sts, place next 14 (14, 18, 20) sts on holder for pocket lining, p8 (10, 14, 16), place next 14 (14, 18, 20) sts on holder for second pocket lining, p across rem 10 (19, 24, 26) sts, then work underpanel in St st and garter st as est to end of row. Cont in patts as est, and casting on 14 (14, 18, 20) sts at both pocket sections to replace sts on holders. *Next row:* (RS) Working both underpanel sections either side of back as est, beg "seam-

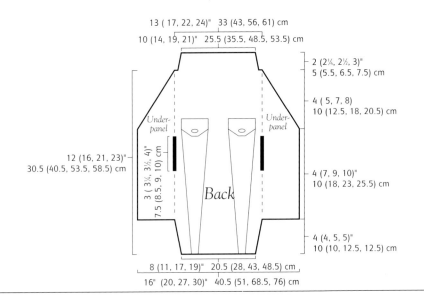

13 (17, 22, 24)" 33 (43, 56, 61) cm

10 (14, 19, 21)" 25.5 (35.5, 48.5, 53.5) cm

2 (2¼, 2½, 3)"
5 (5.5, 6.5, 7.5) cm

4 (5, 7, 8)"
10 (12.5, 18, 20.5) cm

Under-panel

Under-panel

12 (16, 21, 23)"
30.5 (40.5, 53.5, 58.5) cm

3 (3¼, 3½, 4)"
7.5 (8.5, 9, 10) cm

Back

4 (7, 9, 10)"
10 (18, 23, 25.5) cm

4 (4, 5, 5)"
10 (10, 12.5, 12.5) cm

8 (11, 17, 19)" 20.5 (28, 43, 48.5) cm

16" (20, 27, 30)" 40.5 (51, 68.5, 76) cm

ing" pattern by working the 56 (76, 98, 108) sts of back section as follows: k10 (19, 24, 26), pm, p14 (14, 18, 20), pm, k8 (10, 14, 16), pm, p14 (14, 18, 20), pm, k10 (19, 24, 26). *Next row:* (WS) Work garter st and St st of underpanel, then p10 (19, 24, 26), sl m, k14 (14, 18, 20), sl m, p8 (10, 14, 16), sl m, k14 (14, 18, 20), sl m, p10, (19, 24, 26), then work St st and garter st patts of under-panel.

Rep last two rows, remove m between the back panel sts leaving the two original m of underpanel sections in place. *At the same time,* shape "seam-ing" pattern by working in est patts to 1 st before back pan-els of Reverse St st, M1, k1, p2tog, p to last 2 purl sts, p2tog, k1, M1 every 8 (6, 14, 12) rows 3 (5, 3, 3) times, then every 10 (8, 16, 14) rows 2 (5, 2, 4) times.

Leg openings: Complete 28 (36, 42, 56) rows in est patts, then divide work for leg open-ings. On RS row, work in patts as est to first m. Attach a sec-ond ball of yarn and work to second m. Attach a third ball of yarn and work to end. Work each section separately through row 46 (56, 64, 80). Rejoin and cont in patts as est to row 50 (80, 106, 120). At this point, work all sts outside m in garter st. Beg on row 56 (84, 112, 126), BO 9 (12, 16, 18) sts at beg of next 2 rows– 56 (76, 98, 108) sts rem. Work garter st border on first and last 3 sts of rem sts. Dec 1 st each edge every other row 6 (12, 4, 4) times then every fourth row 3 (0, 5, 5) times— 38 (52, 80, 90) sts. On row 80 (110, 144, 158) work all sts in garter st. Work to a total of 84 (114, 148, 162) rows. BO all sts in garter st.

FINISHING
Pocket lining: (Make 2) Place 14 (14, 18, 20) sts from holder on smaller size needle and work 20 (20, 22, 24) rows in St st. BO. Sew lining in place to inside of back. ***Pocket flaps:*** With smaller size needles CO 15 (15, 19, 21) sts. Work 2 (2, 4, 4) rows in garter st. Cont in garter st, dec 1 st each edge every other row 5 (5, 6, 7) times. *At the same time,* when 7 (7, 9, 9) sts rem, work button-hole row as follows: K3 (3, 4, 4), yo, k2tog, k2 (2, 3, 3). BO 5 (5, 7, 7) sts. ***Leg openings:*** With dpn, pick up 26 (30, 30, 34) sts evenly around leg open-ings. Work 6 rows in circ garter st. BO all sts. ***Buttons:*** Sew buttons opposite button-holes on front and under but-tonholes on pocket flaps. Wash and dry garment. Steam lightly to shape.

MATISSE

Did you know that
greyhounds were the
very first dogs to appear
in human works of art?
So I was a natural to
model this artfully
warm creation.
It's a perfect design for
a large, short-haired
dog like me, and
a great improvement
over those little canvas
numbers I used to wear
at the race track.

Native American-Inspired Blanket Sweater

Inspired by the bold colors and patterning of Native American saddle blankets, the low neck of this sweater suggests a blanket draped over the shoulders. The attached I-cord trim further emphasizes the clean lines. Intarsia and jacquard color work, as well as edge treatments, make this design appropriate for the intermediate to experienced knitter.

SIZE	FINISHED SIZE	YARN	NEEDLES	NOTIONS
S (M, L, XL) to fit chest 14 (16, 22, 26)" (35.5 [40.5, 56, 66] cm).	15½ (19, 24, 29)" (39.5 [48.5, 61, 73.5] cm) chest circumference; 11 (15, 20, 22)" (28 [38, 51, 56] cm) length. Sweater shown is Large, 24" (61 cm) chest.	Bulky weight yarn, approximately 120 (150, 200, 250) yd (110 [138, 183, 229] m) fiery red (A); 85 (85, 100, 125) yd (78 [78, 92, 115] m) black (B); 65 (65, 75, 75) yd (60 [60, 69, 69] m) each flannel gray (C), thrush (D) and natural (E).	Size 9 (5.5 mm); two size 6 (4 mm) double-pointed needles (dpn). Adjust needle sizes if necessary to obtain the correct gauge.	Bulky yarn bobbins; crochet hook size H/8 (5 mm). **GAUGE** 16 sts and 22 rows = 4" (10 cm) on size 9 (5.5 mm) needles in St st.

Native American-Inspired Blanket Sweater

NOTE

We used Manos del Uruguay hand-spun, kettle-dyed wool (see Yarns, page 94).

BACK

With size 9 (5.5 mm) needles, CO 48 (56, 72, 84) sts. Follow Chart A, beg with row 1 and working intarsia and jacquard colorwork as shown. Begin dec as shown on chart, starting with row 42 (61, 89, 95). When chart is completed and back measures 11 (15, 20, 22)" (28 [38, 51, 56] cm), BO rem 38 (40, 48, 56) sts.

UNDERPANEL

With size 9 needles, CO 4 sts. Inc 1 st each edge every other row 0 (5, 4, 7) times, then every third row 5 (3, 6, 7) times for a total of 14 (20, 24, 32) sts. Work even to 3½ (4, 6, 7)" (9 [10, 15, 18] cm). *At the same time,* work a single diamond motif as indicated on Chart B, beg on row 11 of underpanel and centering motif between existing stitches. When work measures 7½ (11, 16, 17)" (19 [28, 40.5, 43] cm) from CO edge, BO all sts.

FINISHING

I-cord and attached I-cord edge treatment: With color B and two size 6 (4mm) dpn, work I-cord as follows (see Glossary, page 15, for illustration): CO 3 sts, k3, do not turn work but slide stitches to the opposite end of needle and knit, pulling yarn across back of work to knit first st. Rep this row until work measures 2" (5 cm). Continue working I-cord as established *except* at the end of row pick up 1 st along lower edge of back. Work next row as before, knitting last 2 sts tog, pick up 1 more st at end of row. Cont attaching the I-cord across entire lower edge of back, picking up 1 st for each st on garment. Work 2" (5 cm) more in regular

I-cord (do not attach to sweater). Bind off. Work attached I-cord along side edges of back, leaving 2" (5 cm) of unattached I-cord at lower edge and finishing I-cord even with neck edge. **Note:** To pick up sts evenly along vertical edges, **do not** pick up one I-cord st for each garment st, but skip approximately every fourth stitch to keep edge from stretching.

Sew underpanel to back along vertical edges, slip-stitching underpanel at inside edge of I-cord and leaving a 3 (3½, 3½, 4)" (7.5 [9, 9, 10] cm) leg opening 3½ (4, 6, 7)" (9 [10, 15, 17.5] cm) from neck opening. (This should correspond with the point where underpanel reaches its full width.) With color B, work 1 row single crochet along inner edges of leg openings. *Neckband:* With size 6 dpn and color B, work 2½" (6.5 cm) in I-cord.

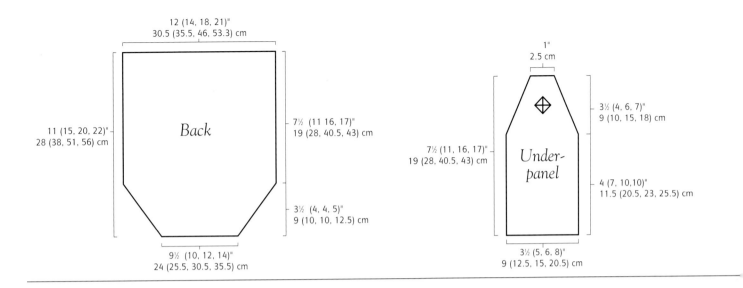

12 (14, 18, 21)"
30.5 (35.5, 46, 53.3) cm

Back

11 (15, 20, 22)"
28 (38, 51, 56) cm

7½ (11 16, 17)"
19 (28, 40.5, 43) cm

3½ (4, 4, 5)"
9 (10, 10, 12.5) cm

9½ (10, 12, 14)"
24 (25.5, 30.5, 35.5) cm

1"
2.5 cm

Under-panel

3½ (4, 6, 7)"
9 (10, 15, 18) cm

7½ (11, 16, 17)"
19 (28, 40.5, 43) cm

4 (7, 10,10)"
11.5 (20.5, 23, 25.5) cm

3½ (5, 6, 8)"
9 (12.5, 15, 20.5) cm

Starting at center front of underpanel, work attached I-cord evenly around neck edge, then work an additional 2½" (6.5 cm) in regular I-cord. Bind off. Cross one end of I-cord over the other and tack in place at center front. Cross one end of I-cord over the other at each side of lower back edges and tack in place. Weave in all loose ends to WS of work.

"The more I know about people, the better I like my dog."

—Mark Twain

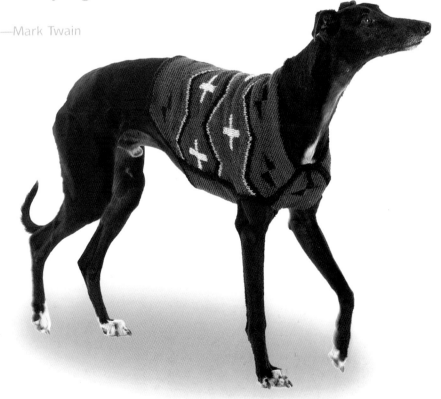

Chart A: Native American - Inspired Blanket Sweater

Key: Native American - Inspired Blanket Sweater

- A - fiery red
- B - black
- C - flannel gray
- D - thrush
- E - natural
- Knit on RS; p on WS using appropriate color as shown on chart

Chart B - motif for underpanel

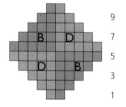

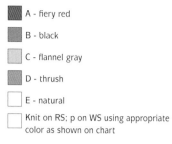

Natural Dog Treats

Natural Dog Treats This recipe for homemade natural dog treats comes to us courtesy of Blue Hill Dog & Cat Shop on Main Street in Longmont, Colorado, where owner Diane Oldfield and baker Kathie Lucero pamper the pets of the Rocky Mountain Front Range. Kathie, who is also a knitter, says that these all-natural, nutrient-rich dog cookies are suitable for all dogs, including those with allergies. The treats can be stored for several months, thanks to long, slow baking, and also freeze well, Kathie says.

Mr. McGregor's Garden Medley

Ingredients

4 cups spelt flour
1 cup quinoa flour
2 tablespoons quinoa grain
2 tablespoons flaxseed meal
1 egg
¼ cup unrefined safflower oil
1 cup grated carrots
¼ cup parsley
1 tablespoon garlic powder
1 cup water

Mix all ingredients and roll out to desired thickness (approximately ¼" works well). Use any cookie cutter to cut out shapes. Bake at 200°F for 2 hours.

BAXTER

I'm Baxter, a terrier
mix of uncertain
parentage and firmly
held beliefs. I think all
dogs should be able
to wear coats and
sweaters, get up on
chairs, and chase balls
until they fall down
from exhaustion. I
may be vertically
challenged, but when
the call came to model
this Aran sweater, hey,
I was the Big Dog!
Now, where are
my slippers?

Classic Cabled Aran
Sweater This classic turtleneck pullover, for intermediate
knitters, is based on traditional Aran stitches. It is
intended to be somewhat loose-fitting.

SIZE
S (M, L, XL) to fit chest 14 (16, 22, 26)" (35.5 [40.5, 56, 66] cm).

FINISHED SIZE
17 (22, 28, 32)" (43 [56, 71, 81] cm) chest circumference; 12 (16, 21, 23)" (30.5 [40.5, 53.5, 58.5] cm) length.

Sweater shown is Medium, 22" chest.

YARN
Worsted weight yarn, approximately 420 (420, 630, 840) yd (385 [385, 576, 770] m).

NEEDLES
Size 6 (4.0 mm); size 4 (3.5 mm): 24" (61 cm) circular and double-pointed (dpn). Adjust needle sizes if necessary to obtain the correct gauge.

NOTIONS
Cable needle (cn); stitch markers (m); tapestry needle; row counter (optional).

GAUGE
18 sts and 24 rows = 4" (10 cm) on larger needles in a combination of cable and moss sts.

Classic Cabled Aran Sweater

NOTE
We used Chester Farms Cestari worsted weight wool yarn (see Yarns, page 94).

ABBREVIATIONS
BC   Back Cross
FC   Front Cross
FPC   Front Purl Cross

STITCHES
Moss Stitch
(worked over an even number of sts)
Row 1: *K1, p1*; rep from * to * across row.
Row 2: Work sts as they appear.
Row 3: *P1, k1*; rep from to * to * across row.
Row 4: Work sts as they appear.
Rep rows 1–4 to form patt.

Four Stitch Front Cable
(worked over 6 sts and 6 rows)
Rows 1 and 5: (RS) P1, k4, p1.

Rows 2, 4, and 6: Work sts as they appear.
Row 3: P1, sl next 2 sts to cn and hold in front of work, k2, k2 from cn, pl.

Four Stitch Back Cable
(worked over 6 sts and 6 rows)
Rows 1 and 5: (RS) P1, k4, p1.
Rows 2, 4, and 6: Work sts as they appear.
Row 3: P1, sl next 2 sts to cn and hold in back of work, k2, k2 from cn, pl.

Double Cable
(worked over 11 sts and 6 rows)
Rows 1 and 5: (RS) P1, k4, p1, k4, p1.
Rows 2, 4, and 6: Work sts as they appear.
Row 3: P1, sl next 2 sts to cn and hold in front of work, k2, k2 from cn, p1, sl next 2 sts to cn and hold in back of work, k2, k2 stitches from cn, p1.

Trellis With Moss Stitch
(worked over 28 sts and 24 rows)
Row 1: (RS) P5, sl next 2 sts to cn and hold in front, k2, k2 from cn (C4F), p10, C4F, p5.
Row 2 and all WS rows: Work sts as they appear.
Row 3: P4, sl next st to cn and hold in back, k2, p1 from cn (BC); sl next 2 st to cn and hold in front, k1, k2 from cn (FC); p8, BC, FC, p4.
Row 5: P3, *BC, k1, p1, FC*; p6; rep from * to *, p3.
Row 7: P2, *BC, (k1, p1) twice, FC*; p4; rep from * to *, p2.
Row 9: P1, *BC, (k1, p1) 3 times, FC*; p2; rep from * to *, p1.
Row 11: *BC, (k1, p1) 4 times, FC; rep from *.
Row 13: K2, (k1, p1) 5 times, C4F, (k1, p1) 5 times, k2.
Row 15: *Sl 2 stitches to cn

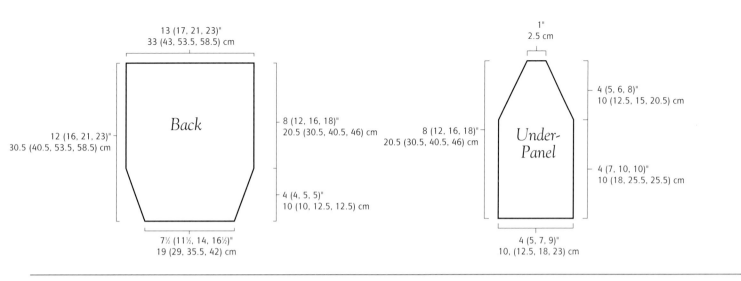

Back

13 (17, 21, 23)"
33 (43, 53.5, 58.5) cm

12 (16, 21, 23)"
30.5 (40.5, 53.5, 58.5) cm

8 (12, 16, 18)"
20.5 (30.5, 40.5, 46) cm

4 (4, 5, 5)"
10 (10, 12.5, 12.5) cm

7½ (11½, 14, 16½)"
19 (29, 35.5, 42) cm

1"
2.5 cm

Under-Panel

4 (5, 6, 8)"
10 (12.5, 15, 20.5) cm

8 (12, 16, 18)"
20.5 (30.5, 40.5, 46) cm

4 (7, 10, 10)"
10 (18, 25.5, 25.5) cm

4 (5, 7, 9)"
10, (12.5, 18, 23) cm

and hold in front, p1, k2 from cn (FPC), (k1, p1) 4 times, BC; rep from *.

Row 17: P1, *FPC, (k1, p1) 3 times, BC*; p2; rep from * to *, p1.

Row 19: P2, *FPC, (k1, p1) twice, BC*; p4; rep from * to *, p2.

Row 21: P3, *FPC, k1, p1, BC*, p6; rep from * to *, p3.

Row 23: P4, FPC, BC, p8, FPC, BC, p4.

Row 24: See row 2.

BACK

With larger needles CO 58 (76, 94, 104) sts. Establish patt as follows:

Row 1: (RS) Work 9 (18, 27, 32) sts in Row 1 of Moss Stitch, work 6 sts in Row 1 of Chart 1 (Four Stitch Front Cable), 28 sts in Row 1 of Chart 2 (Trellis With Moss Stitch), 6 sts in Row 1 of Chart 3 (Four Stitch Back Cable), 9 (18, 27, 32) sts in Row 1 of Moss Stitch.

Work even in patt stitches as established until piece measures 8 (12, 16, 18)" (20.5 [30.5, 40.5, 46] cm) ending with a WS row. ***Shape bottom edge:*** Dec 1 st each edge on next row and on every other row 11 (11, 14, 14) times more—34 (52, 64, 74) sts. When work measures 12 (16, 21, 23)" (30.5 [40.5, 53, 58.5] cm) BO rem 34 (52, 64, 74) sts.

UNDERPANEL

With larger needles, CO 5 sts.
Row 1: (RS) K2, p1, k2.
Row 2 and all WS rows: Work sts as they appear.
Increase 1 st each edge every other row 0 (0, 6, 6) times, then every third row 8 (10, 8, 12) times. Work inc sts into pattern so that center 11 sts form Chart 4 and outer 5 (7, 11, 15) sts are worked in Moss Stitch. Work cable twist as soon as there are enough sts for a full rep. Work even on 21 (25, 33, 41) sts until piece

measures a total length of 8 (12, 16, 18)" (20.5 [30.5, 40.5, 45.5] cm). BO in patt.

FINISHING

Sew underpanel to back along side edges, matching end of underpanel to straight edge of back and leaving a 2½ (3, 3, 3½)" (6.5 [7.5, 7.5, 9] cm) leg opening beg 4 (5, 6, 8)" (10 [12.5, 15, 20.5] cm) from neck edge (at point where underpanel reaches its widest point). ***Turtleneck:*** With dpn pick up 50 (64, 78, 92) sts evenly around neck edge. Work 3½ (4, 4, 4½)" (9 [10, 10, 11.5] cm) in k1, p1 rib. BO in rib. ***Lower edge:*** With smaller size circ needle pick up approximately 94 (118, 140, 162) sts. Work ¾ (¾, 1, 1)" (2 [2, 2.5, 2.5] cm) in k1, p1 rib. BO in rib. ***Leg openings:*** With dpn pick up 24 (30, 30, 34) sts evenly around leg openings. Work 1" (2.5 cm) in k1, p1 rib. BO in rib.

"Whoever said you can't buy happiness forgot about puppies."

—Gene Hill

Key - Aran sweater

C4B: Slip 2 sts onto cn and hold in back; k2, k2 from cn.

C4F: Slip 2 sts onto cn and hold in front; k2 k2 from cn.

Back Cross (BC): Slip 1 st onto cn and hold in back; k2, p1 from cn.

Front Cross (FC): Slip 2 sts to cn and hold in front; k1, k2 from cn.

Front Purl Cross (FPC): Slip 2 sts to cn and hold in front; p1, k2 from cn.

• P on RS; k on WS.

K on RS; p on WS.

Patt rep box.

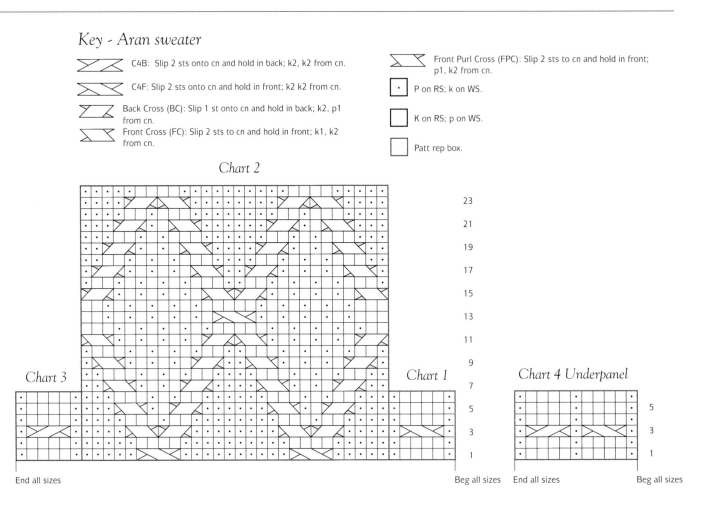

Chart 2

Chart 3

Chart 1

Chart 4 Underpanel

23
21
19
17
15
13
11
9
7
5
3
1

5
3
1

End all sizes

Beg all sizes

End all sizes

Beg all sizes

Natural Flea Control

If you're tired of battling fleas with harsh chemicals, try making your own herbal flea oil, shampoo, and collar. The recipes are courtesy of Sandy Maine, owner of SunFeather Natural Soap Company and author of *Clean, Naturally* (Interweave Press, 2001), a compendium of do-it-yourself formulas for lovely, nourishing soaps and effective natural homekeeping products. Sandy's love for animals is reflected in her natural pet care products.

©2001 Sandy Maine. Used by permission.

Flee Flea Oil

Ingredients*

2 tablespoons peppermint essential oil
½ cup plus 2 tablespoons rosemary essential oil
2 tablespoons white cedar essential oil
¼ cup citronella essential oil
2 tablespoons eucalyptus essential oil
¾ cup olive oil

Mix all ingredients well and store in a labeled opaque bottle. Apply 1 to 2 teaspoons of oil to your hands and rub together, then apply all over your dog's or cat's body every three days during flea season. Wash hands with soap and water after application. Do not get into the eyes of pets or humans. Do not take internally. Every week or two, wash your pet with Flee Flea Shampoo.

Flee Flea Collar

Ingredients*

2 tablespoons peppermint essential oil
½ cup plus 2 tablespoons rosemary essential oil
2 tablespoons white cedar essential oil
¼ cup citronella essential oil
2 tablespoons eucalyptus essential oil

Measure a heavy cotton wick or a natural fiber rope that will tie comfortably around your pet's neck and slip off over its head should it become caught on a branch or fence. Soak the rope in a mixture of the oils (the same mixture as Flee Flea Oil, but more concentrated because it's made without the olive oil base) and let the rope dry for several hours. Then tie the collar around your pet's neck. Resoak the flea collar every two weeks or as needed. Sandy recommends removing the flea collar at night to offer your pet a break from the strong herbal scents.

Flee Flea Shampoo

Ingredients*

2 cups boiling water (or, if you have access to fresh tansy, make 2 cups strong tansy tea and use in place of the water)
¼ cup sodium lauryl sulfoacetate
¼ cup white vinegar
⅛ cup Flee Flea Oil

Mix water (or tansy tea) and sodium lauryl sulfoacetate together and stir until completely dissolved. Let cool. Mix vinegar and Flee Flea Oil together and add to other ingredients. Combine well and store in an opaque bottle, carefully labeled.

To use, place pet in tub and dampen pet's coat. Pour a tablespoon or more of the shampoo into your palm, rub hands together, and lather, beginning in front of the ears and working back and down, until the pet's coat is saturated with the shampoo. Rinse well.

*Ingredients are available through Sunfeather, www.sunsoap.com.

BAYLIE

I know there must be treats in this backpack—I just know it! And I'm not about to hike ten miles before I get one—even in my favorite comfy sweater.

Icelandic Beauty

Inspired by the classic Icelandic yoke sweater scaled down to canine proportions, this sweater draws its details from traditional designs. It works up quickly, and is appropriate for the intermediate knitter. The fit is somewhat loose, as its human counterpart would be.

SIZE
S (M, L, XL) to fit chest 14 (16, 22, 26)" (35.5 [40.5, 56, 66] cm).

FINISHED SIZE
16 (21, 28, 31)" (40.5 [53.5, 71, 79] cm) chest circumference; 12 (16, 21, 23)" (30.5 [40.5, 53, 58.5] cm)

length. Sweater shown is Medium, 21" chest.

YARN
Worsted weight yarn, approximately 180 (250, 300, 400) yd (160 [229, 275, 366] m) light gray (MC); 50 yd (46 m) each deep charcoal gray (A), char-

coal heather (B) and sable brown (C).

NEEDLES
Size 8 (5 mm): straight needles and circular needles (16" or 24" [40.5 or 61 cm] long, depending on size of sweater); size 6 (4 mm): double-pointed

needles (dpn) and 24" (61 cm) circular needles. Adjust needle sizes if necessary to obtain the correct gauge.

NOTIONS
Stitch markers (m); stitch holders; tapestry needle.

GAUGE
17 stitches and 24 rows = 4" (10 cm) on size 8 needles in St st.

Icelandic Beauty

NOTE
We used Brown Sheep Lamb's Pride worsted weight yarn (see Yarns, page 94).

STITCHES
K1, P1 Twisted Rib, Circular Version
(over even number of sts)
Rnd 1: *K1 tbl, p1*; rep from * to * around.
Repeat this rnd for desired length.

BODY
Beg at neck edge with size 6 dpn and MC, CO 52 (66, 80, 90) sts. Divide evenly among needles. Join, being careful not to twist, and place m on needles to denote beginning of rnd and center of under-panel. Work in rnds of K1, P1 Twisted Rib for 3 (3, 3½, 4)" (7.5 [7.5, 9, 10] cm). Change to larger size circ needles and St st, and work yoke patt for each size as follows:
Size 1 (Small): Work 1 rnd in MC. Work Chart 1 (2 rnds) in MC and color A. Work 1 rnd MC, inc 2 sts. Work Chart 2 (4 rnds) in MC and color B. Work 2 rnds in MC, inc 2 sts in first rnd. Work Chart 3 (6 rnds) in MC and color C. Work 1 rnd in MC, inc 4 sts. Work Chart 4 (3 rnds) in MC and color A. Work 1 rnd MC, inc 10 sts evenly spaced. Work Chart 1 in MC and color C. Work 1 rnd MC (70 sts).

Size 2 (Medium): Work 2 rnds in MC. Work Chart 1 (2 rnds) in MC and color A. Work 1 rnd in MC. Work Chart 2 (4 rnds) in MC and color B. Work 1 rnd MC, inc 6 sts evenly spaced. Work 1 rnd color A. Work 1 rnd MC. Work Chart 3 (6 rnds) in MC and color C. Work 1 rnd MC, inc 8 sts evenly spaced. Work 1 rnd color B. Work 1 rnd MC. Work Chart 4 (3 rnds) in MC and color A. Work 1 rnd MC. Work Chart 1 (2 rnds) in MC

and color C. Work 1 rnd MC inc 8 sts evenly spaced. Work 2 more rnds in MC (88 sts).

Size 3 (Large): Work 4 rnds MC. Work Chart 1 (2 rnds) in MC and color A. Work 2 rnds MC, inc 4 sts evenly spaced in first rnd. Work Chart 2 (4 rnds) in MC and color B. Work 2 rnds MC, inc 4 sts evenly spaced in first rnd. Work 2 rnds in color A. Work 2 rnds in MC. Work Chart 3 (6 rnds) in MC and color C. Work 2 rnds in MC, inc 12 sts evenly spaced in first rnd. Work 2 rnds color B. Work 2 rnds MC. Work Chart 4 (3 rnds) in MC and color A. Work 2 rnds MC, inc 8 sts evenly spaced in first rnd. Work Chart 1 (2 rnds) in MC and color C. Work 5 rnds MC, inc 12 sts evenly spaced in first rnd (120 sts).

Size 4 (X-Large): Work 4 rnds MC. Work Chart 1 (2 rnds) in

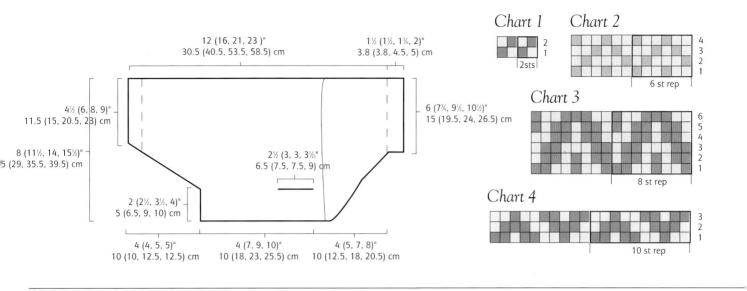

Chart 1   Chart 2

Chart 3

Chart 4

MC and color A. Work 3 rnds MC. Work Chart 2 (4 rnds) in MC and color B. Work 3 rnds in MC, inc 6 sts evenly spaced in first rnd. Work 2 rnds color A. Work 3 rnds MC. Work Chart 3 (6 rnds) in MC and color C. Work 3 rnds MC, inc 14 sts evenly spaced in first rnd. Work 2 rnds in color B. Work 3 rnds in MC. Work Chart 4 (3 rnds) in MC and color A. Work 3 rnds MC, inc 10 sts evenly spaced in first rnd. Work Chart 1 (2 rnds) in MC and color C. Work 5 rnds MC, inc 12 sts evenly spaced in first rnd (132 sts).

Leg openings: When work measures 4 (5, 7, 8)″ (10 [12.5, 18, 20.5] cm) from beg of yoke patt, divide for leg openings. With straight needles knit across 9 (11, 15, 17) sts. Turn and purl back across these 9 (11, 15, 17) sts plus 9 (11, 15, 17) more on other side of m for a total of 18 (22, 30, 34)

sts. Leave rem 52 (66, 90, 98) sts of back on circ needle as holder. Work flat, back and forth in St st on 18 (22, 30, 34) underpanel sts for 2½ (3, 3, 3½)″ (6.5 [7.5, 7.5, 9] cm), ending with a WS row. Place underpanel sts on holder and attach yarn to back sts held on circ needle. Work flat, back and forth in MC on 52 (66, 90, 98) back sts to same length as underpanel, ending with a WS row. Rejoin work and cont in rnds in MC until work measures 8 (12, 16, 18)″ (20.5 [30.5, 40.5, 46] cm) from beg of yoke. Place 9 (11, 15, 17) sts each side of m on holder. Work back and forth on rem 52 (66, 90, 98) sts, dec 1 st each edge every other row 1 (0, 8, 6) times, then every third row 4 (7, 3, 5) times, then every fourth row 2 (0, 0, 0) times—38 (52, 68, 76) sts. *At the same time,* when work measures 10 (14, 19, 21)″ (25.5 [35.5, 48.5, 53] cm) from beg

of yoke, work 4 rows of Chart 2 in MC and color A. When work measures 12 (16, 21, 23)″ (30.5 [40.5, 53.5, 58.5] cm), place rem 38 (52, 68, 76) sts on holder.

FINISHING

Using tapestry needle and matching yarn, fold neckband in half to inside and slipstitch in place. ***Lower edge:*** With size 6 (4 mm) circ needles, pick up 96 (114, 146, 158) sts around lower edge, including those on holders. Work ¾″ (2 cm) in K1, P1 Twisted Rib. BO loosely. ***Leg openings:*** With size 6 (4 mm) dpn, pick up 24 (28, 28, 32) sts around leg openings. Work ¾″ (2 cm) in K1, P1 Twisted Rib. BO in rib patt. Weave in all loose ends to WS of work.

Key: Icelandic Beauty

- A - deep charcoal gray
- B - charcoal heather
- C - sable brown
- MC - light gray
- Pattern rep box
- Working circ, knit all sts in colors as directed. When working back and forth, K all sts on RS; P all sts on WS in colors as directed.

NOTE: Change colors in charts as directed in pattern instructions.

MAGGIE

I love my party dress, and luckily I have party manners to go with it —so my human can dress me up and take me with her to favorite social occasions.

The Party Dress This very feminine, slightly A-shaped

"dress" is soft and sweet, perfect for special occasions.

SIZE	FINISHED SIZE	YARN	NEEDLES	NOTIONS
S (M, L, XL) to fit chest 14 (16, 22, 26)" (35.5 [40.5, 56, 66] cm).	16 (19, 25, 28)" (40.5 [48, 63.5, 71] cm) chest circumference; 10 (14, 20, 20½)" (25.5 [35.5, 51, 52] cm) length. Sweater shown is size Medium, 19" chest.	Worsted weight yarn, approximately 250 (300, 400, 450) yd (229 [275, 366, 412] m).	Size 6 (4 mm): 16" (40.5 cm) circular for smaller sizes, 24" (61 cm) circular for larger sizes; size 4 (3.5 mm): straight and double-pointed needles (dpn). Adjust needle sizes if necessary to obtain the correct gauge.	Stitch markers (m); stitch holder; row counter (optional).

NOTIONS

GAUGE
20 sts and 28 rnds = 4" (10 cm) in Quatrefoil Eyelet Stitch on larger needles.

The Party Dress

NOTE
We used Tahki Sable worsted weight yarn, a blend of merino wool and angora (see Yarns, page 94).

STITCHES

Garter Stitch, Circular Version
Knit one rnd, purl one rnd.

Dinner Bell Ruffle, Circular Version
(multiple of 10 sts)
CO 10 sts for every 4 sts required at finish of ruffle.
Rnds 1, 2, 3: *K7, p3; rep from *.
Rnd 4: *K2, sl 1, k2tog, psso, k2, p3; rep from *.
Rnd 5: *K5, p3; rep from *.
Rnd 6: *K1, sl 1, k2tog, psso, k1, p3; rep from *.
Rnd 7: *K3, p3; rep from *.
Rnd 8: *Sl 1, k2tog, psso, p3; rep from *.
Rnds 9, 10: *K1, p3; rep from *.
Work rnds 1–10 for patt.

Dinner Bell Ruffle, Row Version
(multiple of 10 sts + 3)

CO 10 sts for every 4 sts required at finish of ruffle, plus 3 edge sts.
Rows 1 and 3: (WS) K3, *p7, k3; rep from *.
Row 2: (RS) P3, *k7, p3; rep from *.
Row 4: P3, *k2, sl 1, k2tog, psso, k2, p3; rep from *.
Row 5: K3, *p5, k3; rep from *.
Row 6: P3, *k1, sl 1, k2tog, psso, k1, p3; rep from *.
Row 7: K3, *p3, k3; rep from *.
Row 8: P3, *sl 1, k2tog, psso, p3; rep from *.
Row 9: K3, *p1, k3; rep from *.
Row 10: P3, *k1, p3; rep from *.
Rep rows 1–10 for patt.

Quatrefoil Eyelet Stitch, Circular Version
(multiple of 8 sts)
Rnds 1, 2, 3: Knit.
Rnd 4: K3, *yo, ssk, k6*; rep from * to *. End last rep k3 instead of k6.
Rnd 5: Knit.
Rnd 6: K1, *k2tog, yo, k1, yo, ssk, k3*; rep from *to*, end

last rep k2 instead of k3.
Rnd 7: Knit.
Rnd 8: Rep rnd 4.
Rnds 9, 10, 11: Knit.
Rnd 12: K7, *yo, ssk, k6*; rep from * to *, end k1.
Rnd 13: Knit.
Rnd 14: K5, *k2tog, yo, k1, yo, ssk, k3*; rep from * to *, end k3.
Rnd 15: Knit.
Rnd 16: K7, *yo, ssk, k6*; rep from * to *, end k1.
Rep rnds 1–16 for patt.

Quatrefoil Eyelet Stitch, Row Version
(multiple of 8 sts)
Row 1 and all WS rows: Purl.
Row 2: (RS) Knit.
Row 4: K3, *yo, ssk, k6*; rep from * to *, end last rep k3 instead of k6.
Row 6: K1, *k2tog, yo, k1, yo, ssk, k3*; rep from *to*, end last rep k2 instead of k3.
Row 8: K3, *yo, ssk, k6*; rep from * to *, end last rep k3 instead of k6.

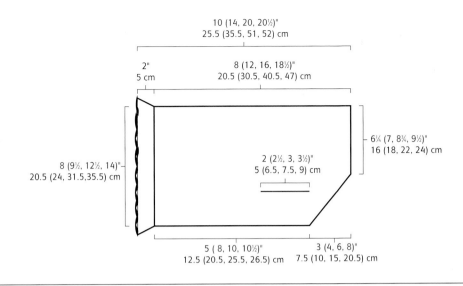

10 (14, 20, 20½)"
25.5 (35.5, 51, 52) cm

2"
5 cm

8 (12, 16, 18½)"
20.5 (30.5, 40.5, 47) cm

6¼ (7, 8¾, 9½)"
16 (18, 22, 24) cm

8 (9½, 12½, 14)"
20.5 (24, 31.5, 35.5) cm

2 (2½, 3, 3½)"
5 (6.5, 7.5, 9) cm

5 (8, 10, 10½)"
12.5 (20.5, 25.5, 26.5) cm

3 (4, 6, 8)"
7.5 (10, 15, 20.5) cm

Row 10: Knit.
Row 12: K7, *yo, ssk, k6*; rep from * to *, end k1.
Row 14: K5, *k2tog, yo, k1, yo, ssk, k3*; rep from * to *, end k3.
Row 16: K7, *yo, ssk, k6*; rep from * to *, end k1.
Rep rows 1–16 for patt.

BODY

Beg at lower edge, with larger needles CO 200 (240, 320, 360) sts. Join, being careful not to twist sts, and pm. Work 10 rnds Dinner Bell Ruffle, Circular Version, ending with 80 (96, 128, 144) sts. Work 4 rnds circ garter st (see Stitches). Begin Quatrefoil Eyelet Stitch, circ version, and work even to 3 (5½, 7, 7)" (7.5 [14, 18, 18] cm) from beg of Quatrefoil Eyelet patt ending with a Rnd 8 or Rnd 16. ***Leg opening:*** Turn, and using straight needle, purl across 16 (24, 40, 48) sts (underpanel), placing markers (pm) either side of sts. Leave rem 64 (72,

88, 96) sts on circular needle as stitch holder. With straight needles, work 16 (24, 40, 48) underpanel sts back and forth in Quatrefoil Eyelet Stitch, row version, for 2 (2½, 3, 3½)" (5 [6.5, 7.5, 9] cm), omitting eyelet sts at edges where a complete patt rep cannot be worked. Place marker either side of underpanel sts to indicate end of leg openings. Break yarn and place 16 (24, 40, 48) underpanel sts on holder. Return to sts on circ needle, reattach yarn and work rem sts in Quatrefoil Eyelet Stitch, row version, for 2 (2½, 3, 3½)" (5 [6.5, 7.5, 9] cm) matching the length of under panel, omitting patt at edges where a complete patt rep cannot be worked. Rejoin work and resume rnds. ***Neck opening:*** Dec for neck opening as follows: Sl m, ssk, work in patt as est to 2 sts before m, k2tog, sl m, complete rnd. Work dec rnds as described every other round 0 (11, 15, 13) times, then every third

round 7 (0, 4, 10) times, eliminating patt bet dec when a full patt rep cannot be completed—66 (74, 90, 98) sts. Change to Size 4 dpn and work 4 rnds in est patt, and then work 4 rnds in circ garter st, dec 2 sts evenly in first rnd. Bind off rem 64 (72, 88, 96) sts.

NECK RUFFLE

With size 4 straight needles, CO 123 (143, 163, 193) sts. Work 10 rows of Dinner Bell Ruffle, row version. BO all sts.

FINISHING

Pin ruffle to neck edge with WS of ruffle to RS of sweater, placing opening at center front and easing neck opening to fit ruffle. Slip stitch in place. ***Leg openings:*** With smaller dpn pick up 20 (24, 30, 35) sts evenly around each leg opening. Work 4 rnds circ garter st. BO.

SCHATZI

Fly-fishing isn't just for
the boys anymore—just
ask any sophisticated
outfitter. "Schatzi," they
told me, "this mossy
green shade will
coordinate superbly
with your human's
waders." Not to mention
warding off that
early-morning chill
along the riverbank
while I keep the
squirrels in check.
Noisy rodents might
scare the fish!

Tweedy Funnel-Neck
Ribbed Sweater Clean-lined and tweedy, this loose-fitting classic sweater is decidedly masculine. It's knitted in one piece, with minimal finishing work, and is designed so that pattern stitches flow seamlessly into place.

SIZE	FINISHED SIZE	YARN	NEEDLES	NOTIONS
S (M, L, XL) to fit chest 14 (18, 22, 26)" (35.5 [46, 56, 66] cm).	18¾ (22¾, 27¼ , 30¾)" (47.5 [58, 69, 78] cm) chest circumference;12 (16, 21, 23)" (30.5 [40.5, 53.5, 58.5] cm) length (not including collar). Sweater shown is Large, 27¼" (69 cm) chest.	Heavy worsted weight yarn, approximately 300 (350, 400, 450) yd (274 [320, 365, 411] m).	Size 7 (4.5 mm): circular, 16" (40.5 cm) for smaller sizes or 24" (61 cm) for larger sizes; size 5 (3.75 mm): set of 4 or 5 double-pointed needles (dpn).	Stitch markers (m), tapestry needle.

GAUGE

16 sts and 24 rows = 4" (10 cm), using larger needles in Seed Rib Stitch II, slightly stretched.

Tweedy Funnel-Neck Ribbed Sweater

NOTE

We used Tahki Donegal Tweed heavy worsted weight yarn (see Yarns, page 94).

STITCHES

Seed Rib I, Circular Version
(over multiple of 4 sts)
Rnd 1: *K1, p1, k2; rep from *.
Rnd 2: *P1, k1, k2; rep from *.

Seed Rib II, Circular Version
(over multiple of 5 sts)
Rnd 1: *K1, p1, k1, k2; rep from *.
Rnd 2: *P1, k1, p1, k2; rep from *.

Seed Stitch, Circular or Row Version
(over even number of sts)
Rnd/Row 1: *K1, p1; rep from *.
Rnd/Row 2: Purl the knit sts and knit the purl sts as they appear.
(worked flat over uneven number of sts)
Row 1: *K1, p1; rep from *, end k1.

Row 2: Purl the knit sts and knit the purl sts as they appear.

BODY

Starting at neck edge with smaller size dpn CO 48 (56, 64, 72) sts. Divide sts evenly among needles. Place marker (m) and join, being careful not to twist sts. Work in Seed Rib I until piece measures 2 (2, 2½ , 2½)" (5 [5, 6.5, 6.5] cm), inc 1 st in each "seed" section in last rnd—60 (70, 80, 90) sts. Change to larger needles and Seed Rib II, placing a second m after first 3 sts. Working sts bet markers in Seed st, and remaining 57 (67, 77, 87) sts in Seed Rib II, inc 1 st after first m and 1 st before second m every other rnd 0 (0, 4, 0) times, then every third rnd 0 (6, 9, 12) times, then every fourth rnd 6 (3, 0, 3) times—72 (88, 106, 120) sts. Work even in patts as est until work measures 4 (5, 6, 8)" (10 [12.5,

15, 20.5] cm) from beginning of Seed Rib II. ***Divide for leg openings:*** On next rnd, work across 15 (21, 29, 33) sts in Seed st. Attach a second ball of yarn and work across remaining 57 (67, 77, 87) sts in Seed Rib II, following est patt. Maintain leg openings by working each section with a separate ball of yarn. Work back and forth in est patts for 2½ (3, 3, 3½)" (6.5 [7.5, 7.5, 9] cm). Rejoin work, break off second ball of yarn and continue in rnds until Seed Rib II piece measures a total length of 8 (12, 16, 18)" (20.5 [30.5, 40.5, 46] cm). Bind off 15 (21, 29, 33) Seed sts of underpanel. Work back and forth in rows on remaining 57 (67, 77, 87) sts in Seed Rib II as follows:
Row 1: (RS) K3, ssk, work in est Seed Rib II patt to last 5 sts, k2tog, k3.
Row 2: P3, work in est patt to last 3 sts, p3.
Work these 2 rows for a total

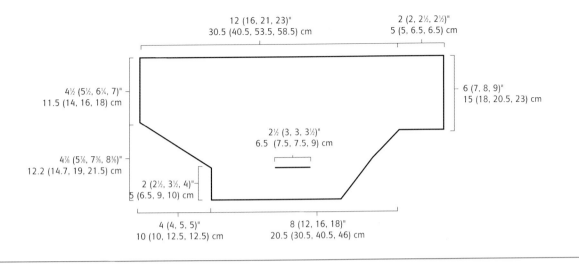

12 (16, 21, 23)"
30.5 (40.5, 53.5, 58.5) cm

2 (2, 2½, 2½)"
5 (5, 6.5, 6.5) cm

4½ (5½, 6¼, 7)"
11.5 (14, 16, 18) cm

6 (7, 8, 9)"
15 (18, 20.5, 23) cm

2½ (3, 3, 3½)"
6.5 (7.5, 7.5, 9) cm

4⅞ (5⅞, 7⅜, 8⅜)"
12.2 (14.7, 19, 21.5) cm

2 (2½, 3½, 4)"
5 (6.5, 9, 10) cm

4 (4, 5, 5)"
10 (10, 12.5, 12.5) cm

8 (12, 16, 18)"
20.5 (30.5, 40.5, 46) cm

of 11 (11, 13, 15) times—35 (45, 51, 57) sts. Work even in patt as est without further dec until Seed Rib II measures a total length of 12 (16, 21, 23)" (30.5 [40.5, 53.5, 58.5] cm). Bind off all sts.

FINISHING

Leg opening trim: With dpn, pick up 20 (24, 24, 28) sts evenly around leg opening. Work 5 rnds in Seed stitch. Bind off loosely. Weave in all loose ends with tapestry needle.

SPIKE

Imagine how it must feel to be a mighty doberman in a chihuahua-sized body. I'm a little terror, and proud of it. But late at night, when They have gone to bed, I like to snuggle on the couch with my favorite knitted blankie.

Arabian Nights
Afghan This lap blanket or dog mat is inspired by a traditional Kilim design interpreted for knitting in a dog-pleasing style.

SIZE

Approximately 24" (61 m) wide and 36" (91.5 cm) long, excluding fringe.

YARN

Heavy worsted weight yarn, approximately 250 yd (229 m) each black (B) and dark orange (O); 125 yd (115 m) cream (C), dark green (DG), light green (LG), tan (T), yellow (Y) and lavender (L).

NEEDLES

Size 9 (5.5 mm). Adjust needle size if necessary to obtain the correct gauge.

NOTIONS

Crochet hook size H/8 (5.00 mm), bulky yarn bobbins, tapestry needle.

GAUGE

15 sts and 20 rows = 4" (10 cm) in Stockinette stitch.

Arabian Nights Afghan

NOTE

We used Classic Elite Montera heavy worsted weight yarn, a blend of wool and llama (see Yarns, page 94).

BLANKET

With size 9 (5.5 mm) needles, CO 88 sts. Working in St st and using the intarsia method (see Glossary, page 11), follow both charts; beg with Chart 1, rows 1 through 100, then work Chart 2, rows 101 through 180. BO all sts loosely using color B (black).

FINISHING

Using a threaded tapestry needle, work in yarn tails, taking care to weave tails into like colors. With color B, work 2 rnds of single crochet around outside edge. Using leftover yarn, cut approximately 360 strands of multiple colors for fringe (strands should be about 12" [30.5 cm] long). With crochet hook, and using 4 strands at a time, fold strands in half, insert crochet hook into single crochet stitch at short edge of blanket, then into center of strands and pull through halfway. Pull ends of strands through this loop and pull gently to tighten (see Figure 1).

Figure 1

Chart 1

Do not BO sts, work chart 2, Rows 101–180 to complete afghan.

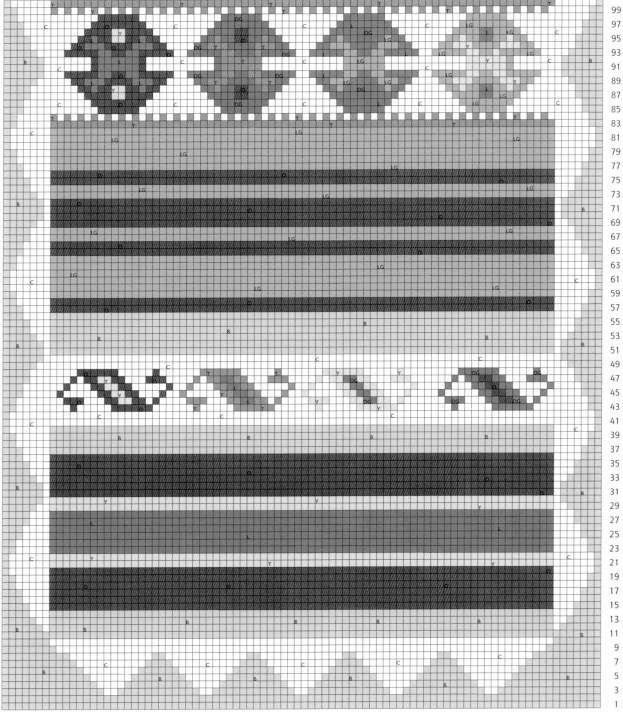

Beg afghan by working this section of chart, Rows 1–100, then follow second section Chart 2, Rows 101–180.

Key: Arabian Nights Afghan

Charts are worked in St st, k on RS; p on WS using colors as indicated.

B black

C cream

LG light green

Y yellow

L lavender

T tan

DG dark green

O dark orange

Chart 2

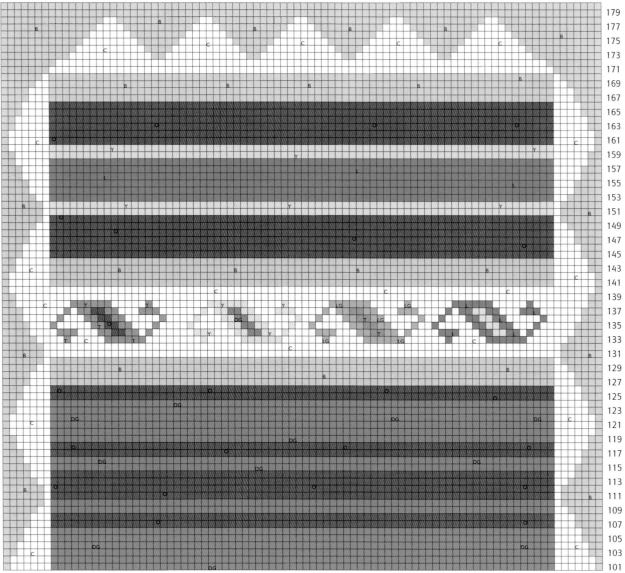

Beg this section of afghan after completing Rows 1–100.

The Courage and Compassion of Service Dogs

Our dogs are beloved for their loyalty, their intelligence, and their sensitivity to our feelings. Most people know that dogs can also aid us in priceless ways; seeing-eye dogs, for example, have long given their blind owners the gift of navigating a sightless world. Dogs can aid those with other conditions as well, whether it's the loss of another of the senses, limited mobility, or other circumstance.

As we come to understand and acknowledge the benefits of interacting with animals, their value only increases. When terrorists attacked the World Trade Center and Pentagon on September 11, 2001, therapy dogs were employed to assist survivors and victims' families throughout the painful ordeal of locating and processing information. The presence of dogs brought light, comfort, and healing into an inexpressibly dark and difficult time.

At the same time, trained search and rescue dogs were bravely entering the wreckage at the attack sites, working in tandem with their heroic human partners to look for survivors and then to find victims. Our hearts were filled with admiration and enormous respect for both human and canine workers.

As we worked on this book, everyone involved wanted to extend a special "thank you" for the work that these service dogs do to make our lives better and easier. In the end, all the dogs we love, in their own way, give us therapy, protection, assistance, and the sweetest of friendships.

To learn more about service dogs, start with these websites:
Guide Dogs for the Blind, www.guidedogs.com
Canine Companions for Independence, www.caninecompanions.org
National Disaster Search Dog Foundation, www.ndsdf.org
Humane Society of the United States, www.hsus.org
American Society for the Prevention of Cruelty to Animals, www.aspca.org

BAXTER

What do dogs do in
Peru? If they're like me,
well, they do the same
things we do at home—
chase rodents and toys
and ride herd on the
humans. After a hard
day of work, it's great
to relax in something
cozy, and on something
cozy too, if I can get
away with it.

Peruvian Treasure

This sweater was inspired by traditional Peruvian caps called ch'ulla. Though the gauge is not nearly as fine as traditional Peruvian knitting, the motifs are adapted from authentic sources, and the bright colors and llama-blend yarn help capture the Andean mood.

SIZE

S (M, L, XL) to fit chest 14 (16, 22, 26)" (35.5 [40.5, 56, 66] cm).

FINISHED SIZE

18 (21, 28, 31½)" (46 [53.5, 71, 80] cm) chest circumference; 12 (16, 21, 23)" (30.5 [40.5, 53.5, 58.5] cm) length. Sweater shown is Medium, 21" (53.5 cm) chest.

YARN

Heavy worsted weight yarn, approximately 200 (200, 300, 300) yd (183 [183, 275, 275] m) purple (MC); approximately 100 yd (92 m) each pear (A), peony pink (B), gold (C), dark orange (D), blue (E), azure (F).

NEEDLES

Size 7 (4.5 mm): 16" (40.5 cm) circular; size 8: 16" (40.5 cm) circular (for larger sizes, a 24" (61 cm) circ needle for the body may be preferable); size 4 (3.5 mm): 1 set double-pointed needles (dpn). Adjust needle sizes if necessary to obtain the correct gauge.

NOTIONS

Tapestry needle; stitch markers (m); row counter (optional); 2 cardboard circles (2" [5 cm] in diameter with approximately ¾" [2 cm] circle cut out of the middle) for making pom-pons.

GAUGE

18 sts and 22 rnds = 4" (10 cm) using size 8 (5 mm) needles in jacquard St st (unblocked); 17 sts and 22 rnds = 4" (10 cm) after blocking; 18 sts and 32 rnds = 4" (10 cm) in circ garter st.

NOTE

We used Classic Elite Maya, a llama and wool blend yarn (see Yarns, page 94).

PATTERN SEQUENCE

Color combinations for each patt repeat are listed after chart number. Work initial set-up rnds for each size as noted in Body instructions before following the chart pattern sequences below:

Size 1 (S): Beg with 14 rnds Chart 1A, and then work foll charts in this order: Chart 4A, Chart 2, Chart 5B, end sweater with chart 1B—53 chart rnds.

Size 2 (M): Beg with 4 rnds Chart 5A, and then work foll charts in this order: Chart 1A, Chart 4A, Chart 2, Chart 5B, Chart 1B, Chart 4B, end sweater with chart 3—77 chart rnds.

Size 3 (L): Beg with 4 rnds Chart 5A, and then work foll charts in this order: Chart 1A, Chart 4A, Chart 2, Chart 5B, Chart 1B, Chart 4B, Chart 3, Chart 5A, Chart 1A, finish sweater with chart 4—101 chart rnds.

Size 4 (XL): Beg with 4 rnds Chart 5A, and then work foll charts in this order: Chart 4C, Chart 1A, Chart 4A, Chart 2, Chart 5B, Chart 1B, Chart 4B, Chart 3, Chart 5A, Chart 1A, Chart 4A, end sweater with Chart 2—122 chart rnds.

BODY

Beg at neck edge with size 7 (4.5 mm) needles and MC, CO 60 (70, 90, 100) sts. Join sts into a circ being careful not to twist, place marker (m) between first and last sts to indicate beg of rnd. Work 8 (10, 12, 14) rnds in circ garter st (knit one rnd, purl one rnd). Work next rnd as follows for drawstring casing: *K1, yo, k2tog*, rep from * to *, end rnd k0 (1, 0, 1) sts. Work 8 (10, 12, 14) more rnds in circ garter st, inc 10 sts evenly in first rnd—70 (80, 100, 110) sts. Change to size 8 (5 mm) needles and circ St st (knit every rnd) and work 1 rnd in MC, inc 5 sts evenly—75 (85, 105, 115) sts.

Size S: Work 14 rnds of Chart 1A (beg of patt sequence).

Size M: Work 1 rnd in color D, 1 rnd in MC, then work 4 rnds Chart 5A (beg of patt sequence) then 14 rnds of Chart 1A, inc 5 sts evenly spaced in first rnd—90 sts.

Size L: Work 1 rnd in color D, then 1 rnd in MC. Work Chart 5A (beg of patt sequence). Work Chart 1A, inc 10 sts evenly in last rnd—115 sts. Work Chart 4A, inc 5 sts evenly in last round—120 sts.

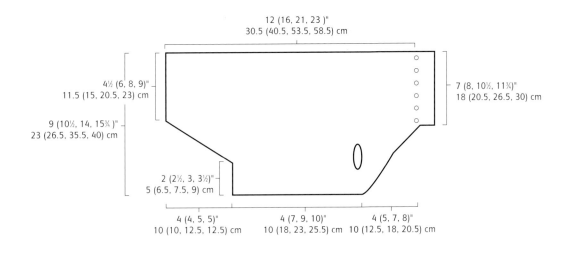

12 (16, 21, 23)"
30.5 (40.5, 53.5, 58.5) cm

4½ (6, 8, 9)"
11.5 (15, 20.5, 23) cm

7 (8, 10½, 11¾)"
18 (20.5, 26.5, 30) cm

9 (10½, 14, 15¾)"
23 (26.5, 35.5, 40) cm

2 (2½, 3, 3½)"
5 (6.5, 7.5, 9) cm

4 (4, 5, 5)"
10 (10, 12.5, 12.5) cm

4 (7, 9, 10)"
10 (18, 23, 25.5) cm

4 (5, 7, 8)"
10 (12.5, 18, 20.5) cm

Size XL: Work 1 rnd in color D, then 1 rnd in MC. Work Chart 5A (beg of patt sequence). Work Chart 4C, inc 10 sts evenly in first rnd—125 sts. Work Chart 1A, inc 10 sts evenly in first rnd—135 stitches. Work Chart 4A.

LEG OPENINGS

Cont chart sequences as listed, when sweater measures 4 (5, 7, 8)" (10 [12.5, 18, 20.5] cm) from casing rnd, work leg openings as follows: On next rnd k7 (9, 11, 13) sts, BO next 10 (12, 14, 16) sts, work in patt to last 17 (21, 25, 29) sts before m, BO next 10 (12, 14, 16) sts, k7 (9, 11, 13) rem sts. On next rnd work in patt, casting on 10 (12, 14, 16) sts above each set of bound-off sts. Work even, following charts until body measures 8 (12, 16, 18)" (20 [30.5, 40.5, 45.5] cm) from casing rnd. Beg working back and forth in rows, BO 9 (11, 15, 17) sts beg

of next 2 rows—57 (68, 90, 101) sts rem. Cont back and forth in rows and patt sequence, dec 1 st each edge every other row 10 (10, 13, 13) times. When body measures 12 (16, 21, 23)" (30.5 [40.5, 53.5, 58.5] cm) from casing rnd, BO rem 37 (48, 64, 75) sts.

FINISHING

I-cord: Using two size 4 (3.5 mm) dpn, CO 3 sts in MC and work I-cord (see Glossary, page 15) for a total length of 30 (36, 42, 48)" (76 [91.5, 106.5, 122] cm). Bind off sts and weave yarn tail through center of I-cord. Thread I-cord through eyelets. Using cardboard circles, make 2 pom-pons (see Glossary, page 14) using scraps of all colors. Stitch pom-pons to ends of cord. *Leg openings:* With size 4 (3.5 mm) dpn and MC, pick up 22 (26, 30, 36) sts evenly around leg opening. Work 4

rnds in circ garter stitch. Bind off all sts. *Bottom edge:* With size 4 (3.5 mm) dpns and MC, pick up approximately 84 (106, 128, 140) sts evenly around lower edge of sweater. Work 4 rnds in circ garter st. BO all sts loosely. Weave in all loose ends to WS of work and secure. Block to size.

"Women and cats will do as they please. Men and dogs had better get used to it."

—Robert Heinlein

Chart 1A: Use colors C and E

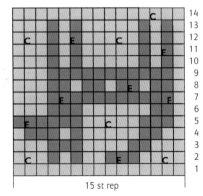

15 st rep

Chart 1B: Use colors D and C

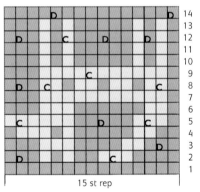

15 st rep

Key: Peruvian Treasure

MC - purple

A - pear

B - peony pink

C - gold

D - dark orange

E - blue

F - azure

Repeat box

Chart 4A:
Use colors B and A

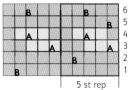

5 st rep

Chart 4B:
Use colors A and F

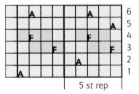

5 st rep

"Outside of a dog, a book is man's best friend. Inside a dog, it's too dark to read."

—Groucho Marx

Chart 2: Use colors F and MC

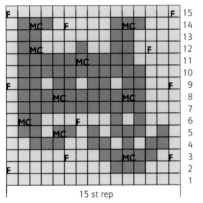

15 st rep

Chart 3: Use colors E and B

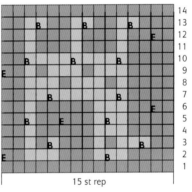

15 st rep

Chart 4C:
Use colors A and MC

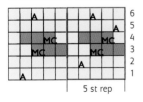

5 st rep

Chart 5A:
Use colors D and F

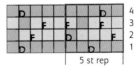

5 st rep

Chart 5B:
Use colors E and A

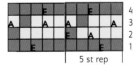

5 st rep

LILY

My human mom is nuts for quilts. Sometimes she tells me, "Lily, you were made from spare parts!" I may be a mixed-breed found on the side of the road, but with this sweater on, I match the master bedspread.

Crazy Quilt Sweater

This gorgeous sweater for the experienced knitter features intarsia colorwork and extensive embroidery embellishment. Use the embroidery to personalize the garment; simple stitches can create elaborate richness.

SIZE
S (M, L, XL) to fit chest 14 (16, 22, 26)" (35.5 [40.5, 56, 66] cm).

FINISHED SIZE
17 (22, 29, 32)" (43 [56, 73.5, 81] cm) chest circumference; 12 (16, 21, 23)" (30.5 [40.5, 53.5, 58.5] cm) length. Sweater shown is Medium, 22" (43 cm) chest.

YARN
Worsted weight yarn, approximately 220 (220, 440, 440) yd (202 [202, 403, 403] m) black (H); 100 yd (92 m) each lilac (A), red (B), rose (C), wine (D), rust (E), peacock green (F), teal (G), royal blue (I).

NEEDLES
Size 7 (4.5 mm). Adjust needle size if necessary to obtain the correct gauge.

NOTIONS
Tapestry needles for embroidery; size G/6 (4mm) crochet hook.

GAUGE
18 sts and 25 rows = 4" (10 cm) in St st.

Crazy Quilt Sweater

NOTES

We used K1C2 Parfait Solids worsted weight yarn (see Yarns, page 94).

Chart A is worked for all sizes through Row 73, and then Chart B from Row 74 to Row 143 for M, L, and XL sizes.

BACK

With color H, CO 58 (76, 98, 110) sts. Work 2 rows in St st (rows 1 and 2 of Chart A). Using the intarsia method, follow charts, working 52 (75, 99, 111) rows even, then work decreases as indicated on charts. When dec are finished, work two rows in color H to complete size. BO all sts.

UNDERPANEL

With color H, CO 18 (22, 32, 36) sts. Work even in St st until piece measures 4 (7, 10, 10)" (10 [18, 25.5, 25.5] cm). Dec 1 st each edge every third row 5 (9, 2, 10) times, then

every other row 2 (0, 12, 5) times, then every row 0 (0, 0, 1) times. When piece measures a total length of 8 (12, 16, 18)" (20.5 [30.5, 40.5, 46] cm) from CO edge, BO rem 4 sts.

FINISHING

Weave in all loose ends on WS, closing any holes that might have occurred joining colors, and being careful to work color ends into like colors. *Embroidery:* Outline all "patches" using chain stitch, blanket stitch, and feather stitch as desired (see Glossary, page 12). Choose colors as you wish, keeping in mind that black (color H) and darker colors seem to work best for outlining. Work floral motifs as desired inside patches. Work small floral motif on center chest of underpanel. Sew back to underpanel along side edges, leaving an opening for legs 2½ (3, 3, 3½)" (6.5 [7.5, 7.5, 9] cm) long, beg 4 (5, 6,

8)" (10 [12.5, 15, 20.5] cm) from neck edge (or at widest points of underpanel and back). *Lower edge:* With size G/6 (4mm) crochet hook and color H, pick 84 (108, 138, 156) sts and work 2 rnds single crochet (sc) evenly around lower edge, then work scallop stitch as follows:
Next row: 1 sc , *skip 2 sts, work 5 dc in next st, skip 2 sts, work 1 sc in next stitch*; rep from * to * end last rep by working into first sc.
Neck edge: Work 42 (60, 78, 84) sc evenly around neck edge and work 4 rows sc. Work scallop stitch same as lower edge. *Leg openings:* Work 20 (24, 24, 28) sc sts evenly around leg opening for 3 rnds. Weave in all loose ends to WS of work.

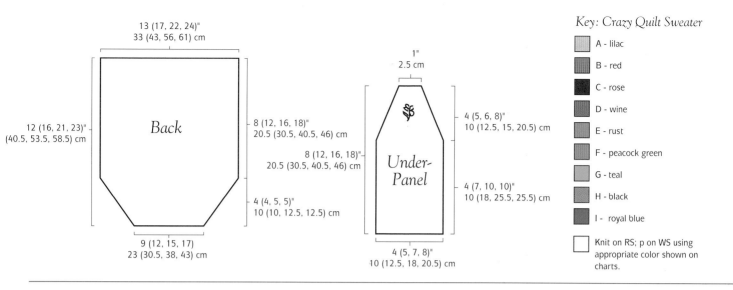

13 (17, 22, 24)"
33 (43, 56, 61) cm

Back

12 (16, 21, 23)"
(40.5, 53.5, 58.5) cm

8 (12, 16, 18)"
20.5 (30.5, 40.5, 46) cm

8 (12, 16, 18)"
20.5 (30.5, 40.5, 46) cm

4 (4, 5, 5)"
10 (10, 12.5, 12.5) cm

9 (12, 15, 17)
23 (30.5, 38, 43) cm

1"
2.5 cm

Under-Panel

4 (5, 6, 8)"
10 (12.5, 15, 20.5) cm

4 (7, 10, 10)"
10 (18, 25.5, 25.5) cm

4 (5, 7, 8)"
10 (12.5, 18, 20.5) cm

Key: Crazy Quilt Sweater

A - lilac
B - red
C - rose
D - wine
E - rust
F - peacock green
G - teal
H - black
I - royal blue

Knit on RS; p on WS using appropriate color shown on charts.

Chart A: Crazy Quilt Sweater

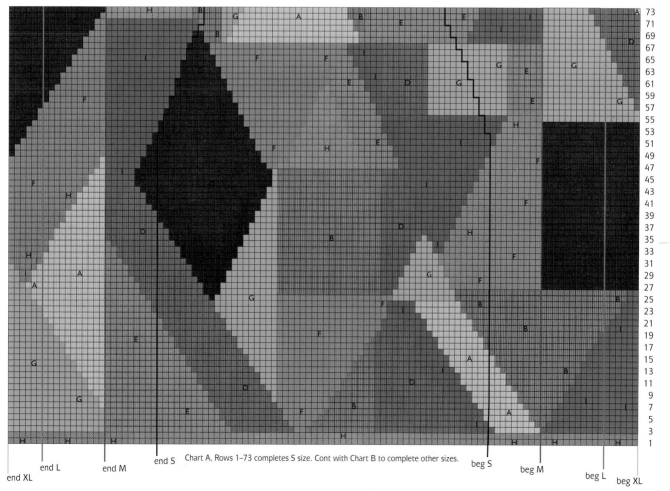

Chart A, Rows 1–73 completes S size. Cont with Chart B to complete other sizes.

end XL   end L   end M   end S

beg S   beg M   beg L   beg XL

Embroidery Suggestions

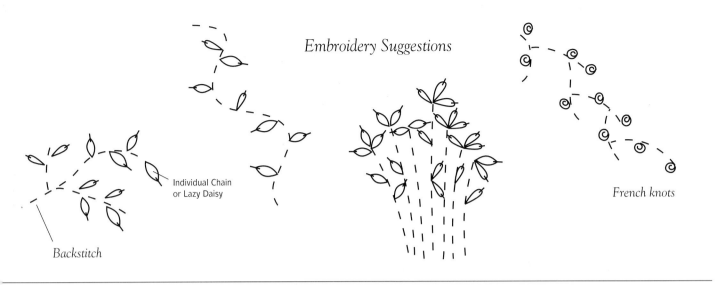

Backstitch

Individual Chain
or Lazy Daisy

French knots

Chart B: Crazy Quilt Sweater

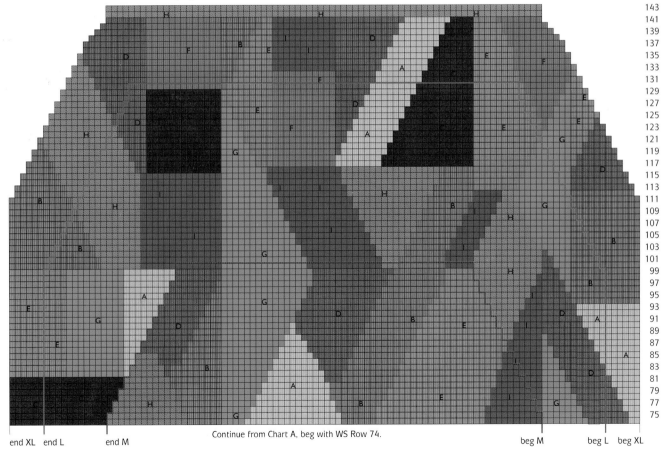

143
141
139
137
135
133
131
129
127
125
123
121
119
117
115
113
111
109
107
105
103
101
99
97
95
93
91
89
87
85
83
81
79
77
75

Continue from Chart A, beg with WS Row 74.

end XL end L   end M   beg M   beg L beg XL

Tips for Three-Dog Nights

Follow these tips from the Humane Society of the United States to protect your pets during the cold winter months. Visit their website, www.hsus.org, for more suggestions.

- Do not leave dogs outdoors when the temperature drops. Most dogs, and all cats, are safer indoors, except when taken out for exercise. Regardless of the season, shorthaired, very young, or old dogs and all cats should never be left outside without supervision. Short-coated dogs may feel more comfortable wearing a sweater during walks.

- No matter what the temperature, wind-chill can threaten a pet's life. A dog or cat is happiest and healthiest when kept indoors. Outdoor dogs must be protected by a dry, draft-free doghouse large enough to allow the dog to sit and lie down comfortably, but small enough to hold in body heat. The floor should be raised a few inches off the ground and covered with cedar shavings or straw. The house should be turned to face away from the wind, and the doorway should be covered with waterproof burlap or heavy plastic.

- Pets who spend a lot of time outdoors need more food in the winter because keeping warm depletes energy. Routinely check your pet's water dish to make certain the water is fresh and unfrozen. Use plastic food and water bowls rather than metal (when it's cold, your pet's tongue can stick and freeze to metal).

- The salt and other chemicals used to melt snow and ice can irritate the pads of your pet's feet. Wipe the feet with a damp towel before your pet licks them.

- Antifreeze is a deadly poison, but has a sweet taste that may attract animals and children. Wipe up spills and store antifreeze out of reach. Better yet, use antifreeze-coolant made with propylene glycol; if swallowed in small amounts, it will not hurt pets or wildlife.

©2001 The Humane Society of the United States

MAGGIE

Just because westies are
the ideal models, it
doesn't mean we're not
real dogs. Like mutts
and mastiffs, we too
dream of big shady trees
full of squirrels and
bones dropping from
the sky, and a human
voice saying softly,
"Maggie . . . Maggie . . .
it's dinnertime!"

Field of Dreams Blanket

A perfect place to curl up and dream, this blanket has all the elements a dog needs to be happy: grass, trees and a sky where clouds turn bone-shaped. Its four identical panels are drawn in a very straightforward manner—just as a dog might paint, if indeed a dog could paint in a representational style. Each panel is given a quarter-turn when stitched together so that the trees radiate out from the center grass.

FINISHED SIZE	YARN	NEEDLES	NOTIONS	GAUGE
Approximately 36" x 36" (91.5 x 91.5 cm) after blocking.	Worsted weight yarn, approximately 500 yd (455 m) wedgewood blue (MC); 150 yd (137 m) each emerald green (A), white (B), teak (C), sandalwood (D), bermuda blue (E), hemlock green (F), tundra (G), and spruce green (H).	Size 7 (4.5 mm). Adjust needle size if necessary to obtain the correct gauge.	Crochet hook size F/6 (4 mm); large-eyed tapestry needle; 9 yarn bobbins.	20 sts and 24 rows = 4 inches (10 cm) using size 7 (4.5mm) needles in St st.

Field of Dreams Blanket

NOTE

We used Harrisville Designs Highland Style worsted weight knitting yarn (see Yarns, page 94).

PANELS

Make 4 panels alike. With size 7 (4.5 mm) needles and MC, cast on 80 sts. Working in St st, follow chart for 108 rows. Bind off all sts loosely.

FINISHING

Weave in all loose ends, being careful to work ends into like colors. Sew panels together invisibly, turning each panel by one-quarter so that all "tree roots" are pointing toward center and matching edges of "grass." (You will be attaching horizontal edges to vertical edges.) *Edging:* With MC, work 3 rnds single crochet (sc) evenly around outer edge, working first rnd as follows: On horizontal panel edges, work 1 sc into each st; on vertical panel edges *work 1 sc into first 3 sts, skip next st*; rep from * to *. Work 2 sts into each corner st. When 3 rnds are complete, work 1 rnd eyelet picot as follows: Work 1 sc into each of first 3 sts, *chain 3, work 1 sc into next st, work 1 sc into each of next 2 sts*; rep from * to * around outer edge. Fasten off. Block or steam as needed.

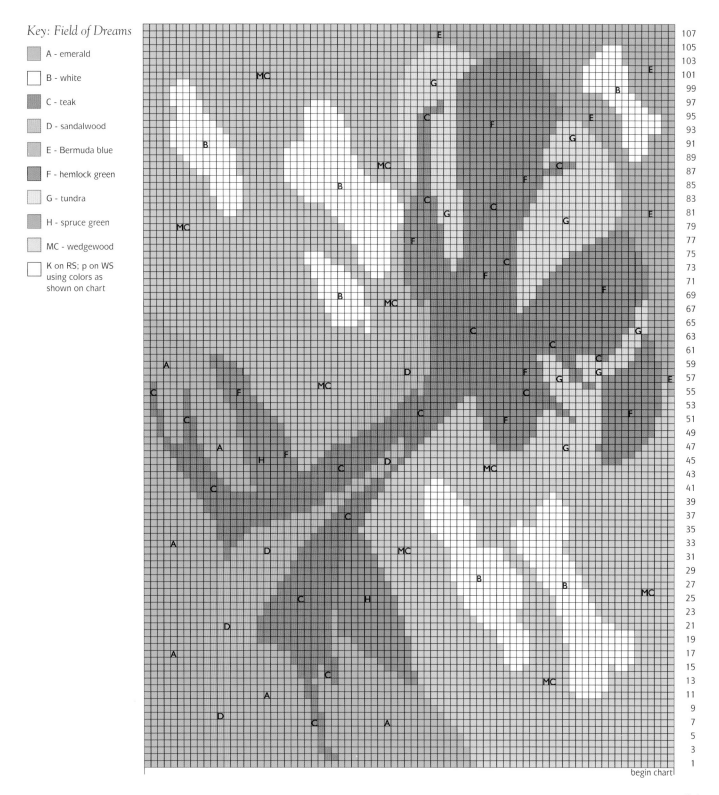

Key: Field of Dreams

A - emerald
B - white
C - teak
D - sandalwood
E - Bermuda blue
F - hemlock green
G - tundra
H - spruce green
MC - wedgewood
K on RS; p on WS using colors as shown on chart

begin chart

JOSIE

A ball of yarn is, well, a ball, right? And my human got to play with so many of them to make me this terrific sweater. I kept hearing, "No, Josie," and "Drop it, Josie," . . . but surely she won't miss just one.

Fetching Fair Isle Jumper
This sweater is very traditional in its technique and yarn. The larger motif is subtly dog-biscuit-inspired.

SIZE
S (M, L, XL) to fit chest
14 (16, 22, 26)" (35.5
[40.5, 56, 66] cm).

FINISHED SIZE
17 (19, 25, 29)" (43
[48.5, 63.5, 73.5] cm)
chest circumference; 9
(13, 17, 19)" (23 [33,
43, 48.5] cm) length

(excluding neck rib).
Sweater shown is
Small, 17" (43 cm)
chest.

YARN
Jumper/fingering
weight yarn, approxi-
mately 150 (150, 150,
300) yd (137 [137,
137, 275] m) dark blue

(MC); 150 yd (137 m)
each light beige (A),
medium beige (B),
medium brown (C),
light blue (D), medium
blue (E), rust (F), dark
red (G).

NEEDLES
Size 1 (2.25 mm):
double-pointed needles
(dpn); size 2 (2.75
mm): dpn. For larger
sizes, use circular
instead of double-
pointed needles.
Adjust needle sizes if
necessary to obtain
the correct gauge.

NOTIONS
Marker (m); tapestry
needle.

GAUGE
28 sts and 28 rows = 4"
(10 cm) on size 2 (2.75
mm) needles in Fair Isle
St st.

Fetching Fair Isle Jumper

NOTE
We used Jamieson & Smith
Shetland 2-ply jumper weight
wool yarn (see Yarns,
page 94).

STITCHES
Corrugated Rib
Working in k2, p2 rib, work
knit stitches in one color
as designated and purl
stitches in second color as
designated:

Rnds 1–4: Work knit sts in MC
and work purl stitches in
color G

Rnds 5–6: K sts in MC, p sts in
color F

Rnds 7–10: K sts in MC, p sts
in color C

Rnds 11–13: K sts in MC, p sts
in color B

Rnds 14–15: K sts in MC, p sts
in color A

Rnds 16–19: K sts in MC, p sts
in color D

Rnds 20–22: K sts in MC, p sts
in color E

BODY
Starting at neck edge with
smaller needles and MC, cast
on 80 (84, 104, 120) sts. Join,
being careful not to twist, and
place m for beg of rnd. Work
in k2, p2 Corrugated Rib following sequence as indicated,
rep rib sequence as needed
until work measures 2 (2, 2½,
3)" (5 [5, 6.5, 7.5] cm). Change
to larger needles and Fair Isle
St st, inc 8 (12, 8, 8) sts evenly
in first rnd—88 (96, 112, 128)
sts. Following chart, work
Rnds 1–26, inc 8 sts evenly in
Rnd 4—96 (104, 120, 136) sts;
inc 8 sts in Rnd 8—104 (112,
128, 144) sts; inc 8 sts in Rnd
11—112 (120, 136, 152) sts;
and inc 8 sts in Rnd 26—120
(128, 144, 160) sts—of first
chart rep.

On second chart rep, inc 0 (8,
8, 8) sts evenly on Rnd 1, then
for 2 larger sizes only inc 8 sts
evenly on Rnd 4—(160, 176)
sts; inc 8 sts Rnd 8—(168, 184)

sts; inc 8 sts Rnd 11—(176,
192) sts; and *for largest size
only,* inc 16 sts on Rnd 26
(208 sts).

Work even on 120 (136, 176,
208) sts until piece measures
4 (5, 7, 8)" (10 [12.5, 18, 20.5]
cm) from beg of Fair Isle St st.
On next rnd, work first 14 (18,
25, 28) sts in patt as est, CO
10 sts for steek, cont in patt
until 14 (18, 25, 28) sts rem,
CO 10 sts for second steek,
work to end of rnd. Work even
on 140 (156, 196, 228) sts,
working Fair Isle patt as est
and working steek sts in alternating colors on 2-color rnds
and as a stripe on single-color
rnds. When steek measures 2½
(3, 3½, 3½)" (6.5 [7.5, 9, 9] cm),
BO steek sts and cont to work
even in patt on 120 (136, 176,
208) Fair Isle sts until body
measures 8 (12, 15, 17)" (20.5
[30.5, 38, 43] cm) from beg of
Fair Isle. Change to corrugated rib sequence and work in

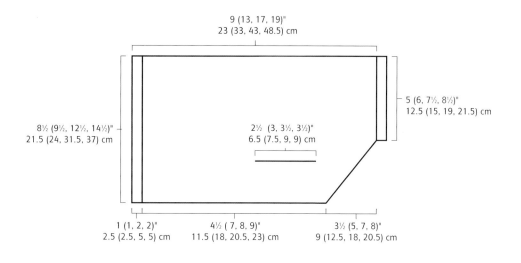

9 (13, 17, 19)"
23 (33, 43, 48.5) cm

5 (6, 7½, 8½)"
12.5 (15, 19, 21.5) cm

8½ (9½, 12½, 14½)"
21.5 (24, 31.5, 37) cm

2½ (3, 3½, 3½)"
6.5 (7.5, 9, 9) cm

1 (1, 2, 2)"
2.5 (2.5, 5, 5) cm

4½ (7, 8, 9)"
11.5 (18, 20.5, 23) cm

3½ (5, 7, 8)"
9 (12.5, 18, 20.5) cm

rib for 1 (1, 2, 2)" (2.5 [2.5, 5, 5] cm). BO all sts.

FINISHING

Weave in all yarn ends. Cut steeks lengthwise down the center and trim to a width of 2 sts each side. Using a single strand of yarn threaded through a tapestry needle, overcast steek edges neatly in place to WS of work. With size 1 (2.25 mm) needles and MC, pick up 36 (40, 48, 48) sts evenly around leg opening and work in k2, p2 rib for ¾ (¾, 1, 1)" (2 [2, 2.5, 2.5] cm). BO. Steam or block as needed.

Key: Fair Isle Jumper

MC - dark blue

A - light beige

B - medium beige

C - medium brown

D - light blue

E - medium blue

F - rust

G - dark red

patt repeat

knit on RS in appropriate color

Chart: Fair Isle Jumper

8 st rep

Where would a dog curl up to read, given the chance? Our dog friends, paws down, voted for this classy cushion. Books? Their taste ran the gamut from *Go Dog, Go* to *Hound of the Baskervilles.* But please, no shaggy dog stories.

Folk Art Plush
Pillow This pillow cover is inspired by American hooked rug designs of the middle to late 1800s, which often glorified treasured pets in a most charming manner.

FINISHED SIZE	YARN	NEEDLES	NOTIONS	GAUGE
24" x 36" (61 x 91.5 cm).	Bulky weight yarn, approximately 400 yd (366 m) teal (A), 150 yd (137 m) each berry (B), black (C), tussock (D), mountain green (E), forest (F), gold-stone (G).	Size 9 (5.5 mm). Adjust needle size if necessary to obtain the correct gauge.	20" (51 cm) or 22" (56 cm) zipper; 24" x 36" (61 x 91.5 cm) oval dog pillow; 7 bulky yarn bobbins; tapestry needle.	16 sts and 20 rows = 4" (10 cm) in St st.

Folk Art Plush Pillow

NOTE

We used Baabajoe's Wool Company Woolpak 14-ply yarns (see Yarns, page 94).

PILLOW TOP

With size 9 (5.5 mm) needles and color A, CO 48 sts. Using the intarsia method (see Glossary, page 11) follow charts 1A and then 1B for shaping and color placement. Work Chart 1A, rows 1 through 90, shaping pillow by casting on sts at beg of row as indicated. Complete pillow using Chart 1B, working rows 91–180, binding off sts at beg of row as indicated to mirror pillow shaping. After finishing 180 rows, BO rem 48 sts. Duplicate st (see Glossary, page 14) can be used to cover small items in patterns, such as dog's eye and highlights. *Note:* If your pet's pillow is rectangular instead of oval, CO 96 sts and work all 180 rows even.

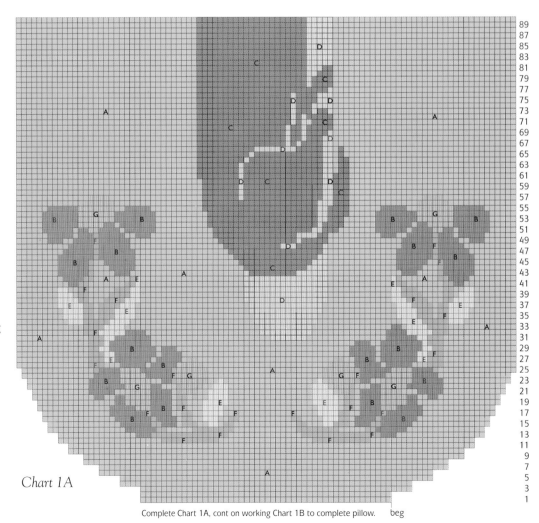

Chart 1A

Complete Chart 1A, cont on working Chart 1B to complete pillow.   beg

Key: Folk Art Pillow

☐ K on RS: p on WS using appropriate colors

☐ A - teal

☐ B - berry

☐ C - black

☐ D - tussock

☐ E - mountain green

☐ F - forest

☐ G - goldstone

Chart 1B

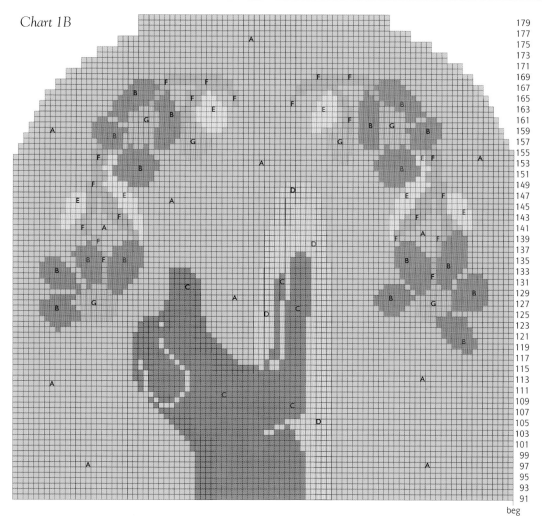

179
177
175
173
171
169
167
165
163
161
159
157
155
153
151
149
147
145
143
141
139
137
135
133
131
129
127
125
123
121
119
117
115
113
111
109
107
105
103
101
99
97
95
93
91
beg

PILLOW BOTTOM

With size 9 (5.5 mm) needles and color A, CO 48 stitches. Following shaping as shown on pillow top charts, work St st in 12-row stripe patt increments as follows: color A, B, D, E, F, G, C. Repeat patt sequence once more, then end with 12 rows color A—180 rows. BO rem 48 sts.

FINISHING

Weave in all loose ends, being careful to work yarn tails into like colors. Sew front to back, right sides together, leaving a 20″ (51 cm) or 22″ (56 cm) opening on bottom side edge for zipper. Sew in zipper by hand using matching thread (see Glossary, page 15). Place pillow inside, smoothing knit cover to fit; close zipper.

UNNAMED PUPPY

Okay, so when I'm too big for this stocking, they'll fill it with treats and chews and toys every year. Right? Or my name isn't . . . um . . . isn't . . . whatever they end up naming me!

Bigfoot Christmas Stocking

Designed to hold plenty of biscuits and toys, this traditional stocking features motifs to delight dogs. The Fair Isle color work and short-row heel shaping make this pattern appropriate for the intermediate to experienced knitter.

FINISHED SIZE	YARN	NEEDLES	NOTIONS	GAUGE
Approximately 8" (20 cm) wide, 17" (43 cm) from top to base of heel, 13" (33 cm) from base of heel to tip of toe.	Worsted weight yarn, approximately 150 yd (138 m) each dark green (A), red (B) and natural (C).	Size 7 (4.5 mm): 16" (40.5 cm) circular and double-pointed needles (dpn). Adjust needle size if necessary to obtain the correct gauge.	Stitch markers (m); large stitch holder; tapestry needle; crochet hook size H/8 (5mm).	19 sts and 24 rows = 4" (10 cm) on size 7 (4.5mm) needles in St st.

Bigfoot Christmas Stocking

NOTE

We used Mission Falls 1824 wool yarn (see Yarns, page 94).

STOCKING

Hem facing: With size 7 (4.5 mm) circ needle and color A, CO 80 sts. Place m at beg of rnd and join, being careful not to twist. Work in St st rnds (k every rnd) until work measures 2" (5 cm). *Cuff:* Change to color C and work 4 rnds in circ garter st (knit one rnd, purl one rnd), then 1¾" (4.5 cm) in St st, then another 4 rnds in circ garter stitch. *Leg:* Work Chart 1, beg with rnd 1 and working through rnd 17 using colors as shown. Work 2 rnds of Chart 4 using colors B and A. Work rnds 1 through 21 of Chart 2 in colors as shown. Work 2 rnds of Chart 4 using colors A and C. Work rnds 1 through 24 of Chart 3 in colors as shown. Break yarn.

HEEL

Heel flap: Sl 20 sts from left needle to empty dpn. Turn, attach color B and using a second dpn, purl across these 20 sts (to m), temporarily remove m and purl 20 more sts from circ needle for a total of 40 sts. Place rem 40 sts on stitch holder to be worked later.
Row 1: (RS) Sl 1 wyb, knit across rem 39 sts.
Row 2: Sl 1 wyf, purl across rem 39 sts.
Rep these 2 rows until heel flap measures 3" (7.5 cm), ending with a RS row. *Turn heel:* On next row (WS) purl 20 sts to center, p2, p2tog, p1, turn. Sl 1, k5, ssk, k1, turn. Sl 1, p6, p2tog, p1, turn. Sl 1, k7, ssk, k1, turn. Cont in this manner, slipping first st and working one more st each time before turning work, until all sts are worked, ending with a RS row (22 sts). Break color B.

FOOT

With circ needle and color A, beg along side edge of heel, pick up 10 sts, pm, knit across 40 sts from holder, pm, pick up 10 more sts along second side edge, knit across 11 sts from dpn, pm (end of round), knit across rem 11 sts (82 sts). Knit one rnd. On next rnd, knit to 2 sts before first m, k2tog, knit to second m, sl m, ssk, knit to end of rnd (80 sts). Work even on 80 sts until foot measures 8½" (21 cm) from base of heel. Work 2 rnds of Chart 4 in colors A and C. *Shape toe:* Change to color C and shape toe as follows (**Note:** When you begin to decrease stitches, change from circ needle to dpn, working first 20 sts on first needle, 40 instep sts on second needle, and rem 20 sts on third needle.)
Rnd 1: Work to 3 sts before first m (or 3 sts from end of dpn), k2tog, k1, sl m, k1,

The top chart is an alphabet chart for duplicate stitch embroidery, shown as a grid of cells marked with × in a pattern forming letters.

	×			×	×	×				×	×	×		×	×	×			×	×	×			×	×	×		×		×		×			×			×	×	×		×			×		×			×			×

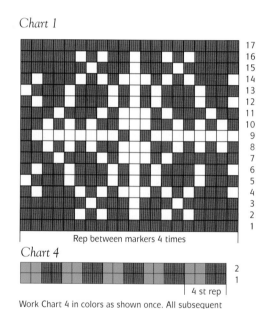

Chart 1

Rep between markers 4 times

Rows: 1–17

Chart 4

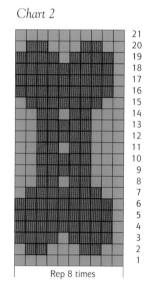

4 st rep

Rows: 1–2

Work Chart 4 in colors as shown once. All subsequent
times replace red (B) with natural (C) yarn.

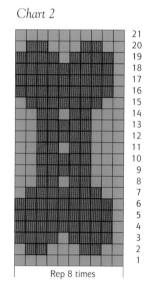

Chart 2

Rep 8 times

Rows: 1–21

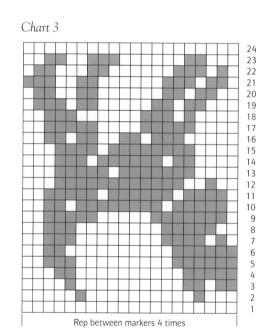

Chart 3

Rep between markers 4 times

Rows: 1–24

ssk, work to 3 sts before second m, k2tog, k1, slip m, k1, ssk, work to end of rnd.

Rnd 2: Work even.

Rep these 2 rnds until 40 sts rem and foot measures approximately 13″ (33 cm) or desired length. Graft rem 40 sts together using Kitchener st (see Glossary, page 14).

FINISHING

Using duplicate stitch (see Glossary, page 14) and alphabet chart above, embroider name as desired on cuff. Turn hem facing to inside and slip stitch to lower edge of cuff. Make hanging loop at center back of cuff as follows: Insert crochet hook into top back of stocking. Holding 1 strand of each color together, pull up through stocking layers and work crochet chain for 3″ (7.5 cm). Join to form loop, fasten off all yarns leaving about 6″ yarn tails. Use tails to securely attach loop to stocking top, weave in loose ends.

Key: Christmas Stocking

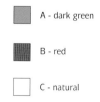

A - dark green

B - red

C - natural

Yarns

Basic Knitted Dog Sweater
Cascade Yarns Cascade 220 (100% wool, 220 yd [201 m]/100g); Small size: 1 skein #7827 bright yellow; Medium size: 2 skeins #8885 magenta; Large size: 2 skeins #10/2413 cherry red; X-Large size: 3 skeins #4146 soft red.

Basic Crocheted Dog Sweater
Cascade Yarns Cascade 220 (100% wool, 220 yd [201 m]/100g); 2 (2, 4, 4) skeins #8892 teal.

Garter Stitch Topper with Easy Embroidery
Lane Borgosesia Maratona (100% merino wool, 121 yd [111 m]/50 g); 3 (4, 4, 5) skeins #8509 blue gray; small amount (approximately 10 yd [9.2 m]) contrasting yarn in similar weight for embroidery.

Soft Basketweave Cardigan
Blue Sky Alpaca sport weight (100% alpaca, 120 yd [110 m]/2 oz); 4 (5, 6, 7) skeins #307 turquoise.

The Jean Jacket
Rowan Denim (100% cotton, 102 yd [93 m]/50g); 3 (4, 5, 6) skeins #225 dark denim.

Native American-Inspired Blanket Sweater
Manos del Uruguay (100% hand-spun, kettle-dyed wool, 135 yd [123 m]/100g); 1 (2, 2, 2) skeins #R fiery red; 1 skein each #08 black, #T flannel, #37 thrush, #14 natural.

Classic Cabled Aran Sweater
Chester Farms Cestari 2-ply worsted weight (100% wool, 210 yd [192 m]/4 oz); 2 (2, 3, 4) skeins natural white.

Icelandic Beauty
Brown Sheep Lamb's Pride Worsted (85% wool, 15% mohair, 190 yd [174 m]/4 oz); 1 (2, 2, 3) skeins #M-130 silver sliver; 1 skein each #M-06 deep charcoal, #M-04 charcoal heather, #M-07 sable.

The Party Dress
Tahki Sable (70% merino wool, 30% angora, 140 yd [128 m]/50g); 2 (3, 3, 4) skeins #1648 mint.

Tweedy Funnel-Neck Ribbed Sweater
Tahki Donegal Tweed (100% wool; 183 yd [167 m]/100g); 2 (2, 3, 3) skeins #879 moss.

Arabian Nights Afghan
Classic Elite Montera (50% wool, 50% llama, 127 yd [116 m]/100g); 2 skeins each #3813 Andean black and #3868 ancient orange; 1 skein each #3816 La Paz natural, #3846 Maquito teal, #3821 sage, #3839 camelid beige, #3825 Kansas sunflower, and #3826 Andes lavender.

Peruvian Treasure
Classic Elite Maya (50% llama, 50% wool, 99 yd [91 m]/50 g) 2 (2, 3, 3) skeins #3052 Peruvian potato; 1 skein each #3087 pear, #3089 peony pink, #3009 San Isidro gold, #3068 ancient orange, #3056 Majolica blue, #3017 azure sea.

Crazy Quilt Sweater
K1C2 Parfait Solids (100% wool, 218 yd [199 m]/100g); 1(1, 2, 2) skeins #1909 black; 1 skein each #1798 lilac, #1369 red, #1219 rose, #1292 wine, #2835 rust, #1539 peacock green, #1681 teal, #1656 royal blue.

Field of Dreams Blanket
Harrisville Designs Highland Style (100% wool, 200 yd [183 m]/100g); 3 skeins wedgewood; 1 skein each emerald, white, teak, sandalwood, Bermuda, hemlock, tundra, and spruce.

Fetching Fair Isle Jumper
Jamieson & Smith 100% Shetland 2-ply jumper/fingering weight (100% Shetland wool, 150 yd [137 m])/1 oz); 1 (1, 1, 2) skeins #FC78 dark blue; 1 skein each #FC17 light beige, #FC45 medium beige, #1287 medium brown, #1280 light blue, #1279 medium blue, #FC63 rust, #FC55 dark red.

Folk Art Plush Pillow
Baabajoes Wool Company Woolpak 14-ply (100% New Zealand wool, 310 yd [284 m]/250g); 2 skeins #11 teal; 1 skein each #02a tussock, #7 berry, #10 black, #12 forest, #27 goldstone, #30 mountain green.

Bigfoot Christmas Stocking
Mission Falls 1824 Wool (100% merino superwash, 85 yd [78 m]/50g); 2 skeins each #018 dark green, #11 red, and #01 natural.

Yarn Suppliers

Baabajoes Wool Company
www.baabajoeswool.com
PO Box 260604
Lakewood, CO 80226

Blue Sky Alpacas
www.blueskyalpacas.com
PO Box 387
St. Francis, MN 55070
(888) 460-8862

Brown Sheep Yarns
www.brownsheep.com
10062 County Road 16
Mitchell, NE 69357
(308) 635-2198

Cascade Yarns
www.cascadeyarns.com
PO Box 58168
Tukwila, WA 98138
(206) 574-0440

Chester Farms
www.chesterfarms.com
3581 Churchville Ave.
Churchville, VA 24421
(877) ONE WOOL

Classic Elite Yarns
300 Jackson St.
Lowell, MA 01852
(800) 343-0308

Harrisville Yarns
www.harrisville.com
PO Box 806, Center Village
Harrisville, NH 03450
(800) 338-9415

Jamieson & Smith Shetland
U.S. Distribution:
Schoolhouse Press
www.schoolhousepress.com
6899 Cary Bluff
Pittsville, WI 54466
(715) 884-2799

Knit One Crochet Too (K1C2) Yarns
K1C2 Solutions
2220 Eastman Ave. #105
Ventura, CA 93003
(800) 607-2462

Lane Borgosesia
PO Box 217
Colorado Springs, CO 80903

Manos del Uruguay Yarns
U.S. Distribution:
Design Source
PO Box 770
Medford, MA 02155
(781) 438-9631

Mission Falls Yarns
U.S. Distribution:
Unique Kolours
www.uniquekolours.com
1428 Oak Ln.
Downingtown, PA 19335
(800) 2552-3934

Rowan Yarns
U.S. Distribution:
Westminster Fibers
5 Northern Blvd.
Amherst, NH 03031
(603) 886-5041

Tahki Yarns
www.tahki.com
1059 Manhattan Ave.
Brooklyn, NY 11222
(800) 338-9276

Bibliography

Gomersall, Susan. *Kilim Rugs, Tribal Tales in Wool.* Atglen, Pennsylvania: Schiffer Publishing Ltd, 1999.

Kopp, Joel, and Kate. *American Hooked and Sewn Rugs, Folk Art Underfoot.* New York: E. P. Dutton & Co., 1975.

LeCount, Cynthia Gravelle. *Andean Folk Knitting, Traditions and Techniques from Peru and Bolivia.* St. Paul, Minnesota: Dos Tejedoras, 1990.

Mountford, Debra. *The Harmony Guide to Aran Knitting.* London: Lyric Books Ltd, 1991.

Orlofsky, Patsy, and Myron. *Quilts in America.* New York: McGraw Hill, 1974.

Paludan, Lis. *Crochet : History and Technique.* Loveland, Colorado: Interweave Press, 1995.

Snook, Barbara. *Needlework Stitches.* New York: Crown Publishers, 1963.

Starmore, Alice. *Alice Starmore's Book of Fair Isle Knitting.* Newtown, Connecticut: Taunton Press, 1988.

Walker, Barbara G. *A Treasury of Knitting Patterns.* New York: Charles Scribner's Sons, 1968.

———. *A Second Treasury of Knitting Patterns.* New York: Charles Scribner's Sons, 1970.

Index